I WAS BORN IN TOONGABBIE

I WAS BORN IN
TOONGABBIE

I was born in Toongabbie

Lorraine Townsend

I was born in
TOONGABBIE

I was born in Toongabbie

I WAS BORN IN TOONGABBIE

CONTENTS

MOTHERS POEM	2
MY FATHER	3
SKEET	6
TOYS	6
SCHOOL DAYS	10
FANCY DRESS	12
MONEY BOX	13
TONSIL DAY	13
CRACKER NIGHT	15
A DOG NAMED HENRY	16
SWIMMING LESSONS	17
FISHING	18
BASE BALL	18
KID'S FIGHTS	19
GROWING UP	20
MY BROTHER JACK	22
BOX OF CHOCOLATES	24
MUM & DAD	25

I was born in Toongabbie

The Depression	27
War Time	28
Coupons	31
Cousin Bulla	32
My Brother Bill	33
Subs in the Sydney Harbour	37
Movie Theatres	38
Myers Bakery Oct 1942	40
A Horse named Peter	42
Dolly	44
Busy Times	45
The Black Smiths	46
A Cow of a Horse	47
The Pony	48
Pommies	50
Wild Ride	51
Back to the Bakery	53
Carthorse named Dolly	54

I was born in Toongabbie

Transport	55
14 Year's Old	57
Apprenticeship	58
Manly Pool Pavilion	62
Day Dreams	63
The Younger Set	64
I used to go to dances at Manly	68
North Manly Football Club	69
Sister's Wedding	70
1945	72
Polio	73
McNamara Frame	75
The Sister Kenny Treatment	76
Wheelchair Run	78
The Challenge	80
Bed Pans	82
A night at the Pictures	83
The Pet	86
18th Birthday Party	87

I was born in Toongabbie

Hospital Visitors	88
Shallow Waters	89
Home for Christmas	90
Dance Challenge	92
Crippled Children's Association	93
Kiss and tell	95
Sand in the face	96
The Train Ride	97
The Royal Easter Show — 1947	98
Finding Work after Polio	100
Village Dry cleaners	101
Courting	102
Marriage 1950	105
Honeymoon	109
First Home	110
The Partnership	114
Work Camp	115
Our First Child	117
Button's	118

I was born in Toongabbie

The Fire-Storm	118
After the Fire	123
Albatross Naval Base	124
Timber!	125
Re-Building	126
A dog named Mike	128
Monday Dec 15, 1952	129
Wednesday Dec 17, 1952	131
Life without Beryl	131
Tasmania 1953	133
Woy Woy	137
New Beginnings	139

I WAS BORN IN TOONGABBIE

Published 2014

1st Addition
All rights reserved Apart from fair dealing for the purposes of private study, research, criticism or review as permitted under the Copyright Act, no part of this publication may be reproduced, stored in a retrieval system or transmitted in any form or by any means electronic, mechanical, photocopying, recording or otherwise, without the prior written permission of the Author Lorraine Townsend
ISBN 978-0-9924151-1-2

Acknowledgements

I would like to thank my father for sharing what I believe to be a great Australian story of his life and times.

I also wish to acknowledge Ian Summers and my brother Greg Rae for giving their expertise in editing this book.

I WAS BORN IN TOONGABBIE

REG RAE

~27th April 1929~

I WAS BORN IN TOONGABBIE

MY MOTHER'S POEM

Don't try to be an Angel

With eye's fixed on a Star

Just try and be the fellow,

That your mother thinks you are.

I WAS BORN IN TOONGABBIE

MY FATHER

My father's name was William Robert Livingston Rae. He had a brother John Livingston Rae, and a sister called Alice Rae; he married Eileen May Knight, who had four brothers Harold, Reginald, Sidney, and Francis better known as Frank, and four sisters Elizabeth, Emily, Myrtle, and Phyllis.

I had three older brothers Alfred George, Bill Robert Livingston, John Sidney, and two sisters Alice Joyce, & Dorothy Jean;

I was the youngest in the family my name is *Reginald James Rae*.

I was born in Metella Road, Toongabbie. I'm told Dad hitched up the sulky to fetch Nurse Ricardo; she was the district nurse for home births.

When I came along I was a sickly baby; I couldn't keep my food down and cried most of the time.

To give my mother a rest, I believe an Italian woman would pat me on the back and say: 'Bruno you little Mongrel! Why don't you shut up, and give your mother a rest?'

One day, my sleep deprived Mother, unable to cope any longer, threw me across the room; luckily Dad was there and managed to catch me.

I WAS BORN IN TOONGABBIE

The district nurse suggested that I be given brown bread, and the white of an egg mixed together, with a drop of brandy.
This mum did, and finally I started to keep food down, and my parents got good night's sleep.
When I was very small, my sister Joyce picked me up and sat me on the veranda railing to see the fire engine go past. I was wriggling about, and fell to the ground, ending up with a green splinter break near the elbow.

As I understand from conversation of my elders, my father worked on the wharves in Sydney and reared a few pigs on his small holding, to sell.
The first I remember is the house we lived in, or should I say squatted in. It was up on top of a hill at Harbord. We had moved to Sydney after my father lost his job on the wharves and the house he was buying.
The story I heard was: The overseer or whatever they called him, said to Dad,
'Bill, I don't see you over the pub having a beer.'
Dad said, 'I have a wife and six kids, and am trying to get the house finished and paid for - I can't afford a beer.'
After that when Dad lined up for work he was never picked.
Its amazing how one working man can destroy another's family for the sake of a few beers.

I was born in Toongabbie

Mum said, 'Dad worked in the mines at Broken Hill until the labours went on strike; this lasted a long time, and because they were on strike he couldn't work
which caused him to run out of money'.

In 1916, Dad was marching in an anti-conscription procession down Pitt-Street with 700 others against mandatory National Service, and he happened to be in the wrong place wrong time. They were mobbed by soldiers, arrested and marched into the Police Station, charged, and spent a night in goal.

Dad once wrote to his father and asked him if he could send him the fare to Adelaide, because he had a job down there at the Post Office, and he would pay him back.

His father sent him a Telegram, ' You got there, you get back'.

Dad said, ' He taught me that I had to stand on my own two feet' and he never took any offence at this.

My father used to carry the old hand push lawn mower and shears over to Queenscliff and mow lawns for 2/- (two shillings). If we were lucky he would come back home with an Apple pie, if they were cooking them.

My mother would work, doing the washing and cleaning house for a Mrs. Fox at Balgowlah.

The Bread Carter used to give us a loaf of bread when he could.

I was born in Toongabbie

Skeet

I had a nickname: my father called me *Skeeter*, later shortened to Skeet. I think it was short for mosquito, as I was small for my age and was always buzzing around somewhere.
I don't know why I didn't grow - I would go to my Aunt Emily's in Undercliffe on Sunday's and have a baked meal for lunch at 12 O'clock, then would run home and have another baked lunch at 1 O'clock.

Toys

Toys were not plentiful, but we were happy with what we had.
 If we wanted to play 'rounders,' better known as 'baseball,' we would find a suitable piece of wood or a branch of a tree, and cut it to size.
Our toys were kites made out of newspaper and sticks. We would scrounge around for old rags for a tail and pick up any string we could find.
Mrs. Croskey, the local storekeeper, gave me an old toy truck she had that advertised steamrollers.
She used to call me 'The Little Professor' as she said the only part of me that seemed to grow was the hair.
Someone gave us a crystal radio set; I think we could only get one station, when you could get the cat's whisker in the right place.

I WAS BORN IN TOONGABBIE

Children under 5 travel free. I was a few years past five when the bus driver started to asked questions on how old I was. Mum said, I was 4 ½ show him your fishers teeth love; I'd give him a big grin.

I was born in Toongabbie

My mother use to sing a shortened version of this song to me when I was young, with a hint of amusement in her voice.

♫ *Little man you've had a busy day* ♫

Little man you're cryin', I know why you're blue,
Someone took your kiddy-car away,
Better go to sleep now,
Little man you've had a busy day . . .

Johnny won your marbles; tell you what we'll do,
Dad will get you new ones right away,
Better go to sleep now,
Little man you've had a busy day . . .

You've been playin' soldier, the battle has been won,
The enemy is out of sight,
Come along there soldier, put away your gun,
The war is over for tonight . . .

Time to stop your schemin', time your day was through,
Can't you hear the bugle softly say?
Time you should be dreamin',
Little man you've had a busy day . . .

Time you should be dreamin', better go to sleep now
Little man you've had a busy day . . .

Music by Mabel Wayne
with lyrics by Maurice Sigler and Al Hoffman 1934
T.B. Harms & Co.

I was born in Toongabbie

William Robert Livingston Rae and Reg Rae

School Days

Except for Alf, (he was the oldest) we all attended St John Catholic Primary School in Harbord, and at the time it had two functions. It was both a Church and a School.
Through the week the curtains were drawn across the altar while school was held. Then, another partition was drawn across the Classroom for the Sunday Service.
They Divided the Classrooms into sections. One section held the Infants (Bubs): first and second. The other section had third, fourth and sixth class.
Fifth Class was held in the open shed, and typing was taught in the little side room.
One Classroom was held in an open sided shed. This stuck in my mind
I think it was because of the laughter I caused, when I was in the Bubs Class. I had to go to the toilet and in those days, my pants buttoned to the front and back of my shirt, and I could not get my pants back on. So I walked up to the open side of the shed waving my pants in the air, calling out to my sister who was most embarrassed, telling her I couldn't get my pants on. She says even now, 'that I was a bugger of a kid'.
When I was young I had a problem with some words that would come out a little funny and my sisters and brothers would laugh at me when this happened. As far as I was concerned it wasn't funny, and I did find that I was affected by their constant heckling.

I WAS BORN IN TOONGABBIE

Dot & William Robert Livingston Rae

I WAS BORN IN TOONGABBIE

FANCY DRESS

Every year we would have a fancy dress ball for us kids till about 9 O'clock then the parents would take over the dance floor.

One-year, mum dressed me up as a 'Barrister' wig and all. It must have caused some chuckles, as I was the only one in the family that had the least interest in learning.

I hated those dances. The nuns would line us up weeks before the dance, and teach us how to dance.

They would line the girls up on one side, and the boys on the other. The girls used to tell each other who they danced with last week, and the girl that had me would invariably point to me and say: 'I had him. whooooooo'. (*I hated girls*)

I had freckles then, and my hair would not stay combed. When I was in second class, an Italian boy named Hugo came to our school. The teacher told him that all new boys had to sing for the class and we all backed her up. He sang "*O Sole Mio*" by Luciano Pavarotti when he had finished the classroom was quiet; we wanted him to sing some more.

Unfortunately the war was on at the time, we were at War with the Italians and it wasn't long before the kids were calling him 'A Dago.'

It was him and me against the rest; eventually he was accepted and everything went back to normal.

(I was about 20 years of age when I saw him again; he was working on the buses).

Money Box

I remember mum telling me once, how I raced into the house out of breath and asked her where the tomahawk was. When she asked me what I wanted it for,
I told her that people were putting money in the Telephone Box, and no one was taking it out.
So Pat and I were going to get it (I must have been very young at the time). When mum explained to me what it was all about, I was glad that I spoke to her before I broke into the Telephone Box.

Tonsil Day

I had a couple of stints in Manly Hospital in my school days. The first was when I had my tonsils out. In the 1930s the operation was done on all children of school age, on an outpatient basis under general anesthesia by general practitioners. We all sat in the waiting room until our names were called, then we would go into the next room and lay down on a trolley or high table.
They would place a Chloroform Mask over our face and tell us to count to ten; it smelt awful. After they removed

I WAS BORN IN TOONGABBIE

your tonsils you woke up from the anesthetic in the next room on a camp style stretcher, with a basin beside you to sick the blood into. Everyone was singing out for mum, but I was determined I wouldn't sing out for mum, I was the only one singing out for Dad. When you finished being sick you were sent home.

The next time I went to hospital, was when I was standing in the middle of a "Razzle-Dazzle" near Manly Beach. My two cousins decided to push it like a swing; I ducked to miss the seat and crawled out on my hands and knees.

But I made the mistake of lifting my head too soon, and it hit me on the back of the head.

My two cousins raced around to my Aunt Emily who was living in a flat not far from the beach at the time, and there was me walking along with blood pouring out of my head. My Aunt bandaged my head, and sent me down to the Ambulance Station they took one look at me, and drove me to Manly Hospital.

The nurses put me into bed, cleaned me up, and told me I was going to have an X-Ray. This invention wasn't very old at the time, and I had never heard of it. They told me it was only like taking pictures of my head. I was still suspicious until it was over. Later they wheeled me across to their little room put me on a table and started to put stitches into my head, and I felt every one of them. I moved when they were putting the last stitch in, and the doctor said: 'Where's that soldier we had here?'

I let him know, in good 'Old Aussie' terms that... 'I was no Bloody Soldier'.

CRACKER NIGHT

Every year on Guy Fawkes Night, we worked together in-groups for weeks before hand, collecting scrub, old branches from trees, or anything else that would burn. When the big night arrived, we would be given our fireworks and all the families would gather around large bonfires, and enjoy the display.
There was no alcohol at these turnouts; people seemed more responsible in those times. Just joining in with the children seemed to be enough fun, and we enjoyed having the adults there. The only trouble we had were kids coming around on bonfire Night at dusk and lighting any unguarded bonfire, then running off.
One time my elder brothers and sisters left me on guard, while they had dinner.
As it was starting to get dark I hid among the branches. Until I heard one kid say to the other, 'have yar got the matches' I don't know who got the biggest fright them or me. Leaping out of my hide-away to frighten them off, I must have been as white as a ghost - I still remember how my legs were shaking. I'm glad I got out of there when I did, or I might have missed dinner. When I told

the family, all they said was 'Yer got a watch out kids are go'n round light'n bonfires and takin' off'.

In 1986 crackers were banned. Manufactures started bringing in larger crackers and rockets with hard plastic cones. I feel that if politicians had have acted with more responsibility, as to the size and type of crackers sold, kids would still be having fun today.
There appeared less parental involvement; and I am told some people who were old enough to know better threw crackers into open windows of cars.
It seems a shame that because of a few irresponsible people, a family get together vanished.

A DOG NAMED HENRY

In 1935, some people who ran a small grocery shop in Queenscliff had some pups to give away.
I was about six at the time, when I asked mum if I could have a dog.
Mum said, 'Yes'.
So I picked out this little black and white cross Kelpie. On the way home, I put the pup down my jumper to keep him warm until, I started noticing fleas coming out of my jumper, and it wasn't very long before I was holding him by the scruff of the neck at arm's length. When I got home mum saw the fleas, and said: 'Quick inside and have a bath'.

Then she put the dog and my clothes in the bath to get rid of the fleas.
I called the dog Henry; He had a track worn in the lawn from the back door, to the front door. His favorite game: was to run to the front door, sneak through the lounge room, and look around to see if anyone was about. If not, he would take off through to the back door. If we happened to see him coming we would wait until he started his run, then sing out; 'Hey what are you doing in here'! He would turn around, and his little legs would go flat out for the front door. The only trouble was he had such momentum up that by the time he got traction on the polished floor he was nearly out the back door anyway. It was a sight to be seen Henry running one way and his body going the other.

Swimming Lessons

I unwilling learnt how to swim at Harbord Baths, from an old fellow by the name of Vaughan, who kept accidentally bumping me into the water anytime he happened to pass me while I was walking around the baths.
I learnt to dog paddle very quickly.
I was never a person to take on organized sport at school. I was more interested in doing my own thing, which was mostly surfing, bike riding and some fishing.

I WAS BORN IN TOONGABBIE

FISHING

I remember once my cousin John Eagan took me fishing off the rocks at Harbord, and wouldn't let me go near the edge, so I had to fish in the rock potholes.
We must have been there for a couple of hours. John caught a small Rock Cod and I caught a large Blackfish that over lapped the sides of a dinner plate (it must have got stranded when the tide went out).
Mum wouldn't believe me, until my cousin told her I was right.

BASE BALL

I went to Harbord Public School for 12 months. That was fifth or sixth class and we had the old Headmaster who used to look after us for our teacher. They wanted me on the football team, and they told me what team I was playing in.
 I said, 'Who said I was playing?'
They said, 'Alright then don't play' and they took the jumper away and gave it to someone else to play.
So I played rounders (baseball); we were playing the Brookvale School at Brookvale Oval. The word got around that Brookie after the game were all going to get

stuck into us, and going to have a fight but it never did eventuate. We got out of the fight, but they did fight with other schools at times, and they were going to go for us. The teacher was onto it too; we were ready for it and we packed up and left.

Kid's Fights

I was never one who liked fighting and avoided one whenever I could. I still managed to have my share, probably because I couldn't help standing up for the underdog.
Other times, it was because the other boy was too persistent. When that happened I gave it all I had, head down with both fists flying, and wouldn't stop until someone stopped it, or we both decided to give up.
One fight I was in, I lost count of the times I got up off the ground. I landed him one; his eyes started to roll and he swayed on his feet, so I stopped and held him and asked if he was all right, he gave his head a shake and it was on again until the teacher stopped us, and made us sit on the verandah.
When we washed our faces he had as much skin off his face as I did.

Later on I found out his brother was supposedly, The Amateur Boxing Champion of Newcastle at the time, and had taught him how to box.

Another time my cousin had a gang. I must have upset him at one time, because he put his gang onto me. When I had my back to the wall of the shed I reached out through the mob and grabbed my cousin by the shirt, and pulled him to me. I had the other fist in the air ready to land him one, when he yelled to his gang to 'let me go.' I had made up my mind if I was going to cop it so was he.

He became a Detective Sergeant in the Police Force (I believe he died in 1986).

I had the same trouble with a boy by the name of Roe, at Harbord Public School. Neither of them ever worried me again

Growing Up

When I was growing up, every now and then you would find when you were short, there was always someone around that was bigger than you, and tried to impress others by pushing you around, so you had to learn how to fight or run.

My mother told me providing you do not start the fight, and he is bigger than you, you are entitled to pick up a piece of 3 x 2 timber and lay into him.

(Luckily, I never had the occasion to).
I remember there used to be a small quarry in Evans Street; it had a steel cable running from it, to the top of a pole across the road. I must have been about eight at the time. I started swinging hand over hand, on this cable towards the other pole. I was out about eight to ten feet, when some kids started to throw stones at me. I turned around and swung my way back, when I reached the Quarry the kids took off into the scrub, with me after them. I lost them in the scrub, so I headed along Evans Street for home. I was just about to pass two elderly people, when one of them started to abuse me and call me a bully chasing those two children along the top of that quarry; and they were rambling on how they could have fallen off and died.
I tried to tell them that they played there most of the time, and what they did to me. When I looked up, all I could see was her mouth going, and I reckoned I had no hope, so I just kept on walking.
I realized she had her audience, and wasn't going to let me take them away from her. She probably was not able to get much attention in her life, and had little to talk about, so when she found something, she wasn't about to let it go.
We used to have a saying Believe none of what you hear, and only half of what you see.

I WAS BORN IN TOONGABBIE

MY BROTHER JACK

I was never a brilliant scholar at school; it was just that I was not interested.
The older sisters were far in advance of me, and one in particular used to ask me to pronounce a word and then laugh at the way I pronounced it.
Then my brother Jack told me once, that he was glad the rest of the College boys did not see me, the way I was dressed; which made me decide that I did not want to grow up like them.
I was more interested in what the workers were doing.
Mother used to say, 'Jack Rae will have a brass plate on the front gate' with 'Jack Rae, Accountant on it; what will you have?'
I said, 'I would have a piece of tin, with 'Reg Rae, Bottle'o on it.'
I couldn't stand people who talk with a plum in their mouth.

Mum showed me a photo of Jack in his College uniform when I was about 20 and said, 'This is the bloke who told you he did not want the rest of the College boys to see you.'
All I could do was laugh at the little squirt. I'm glad mum showed me the photo; otherwise, I could possibly have held it against him to this day. Jack was a

tormenting bugger - he used to stand in the way of my games or knock them over, and destroy my toys.

He was a couple of years older than me, and could out-reach and out-run me. One time I had all I could take, and decided to take him on. Anyway, before I could get to him, He took off up the side of the house. I picked up half a house brick on the way and let it fly. It hit him on the back of the head and laid him out. I got frightened and ran into the house and told mum.

When mum reached him, he was a bit groggy. Mum took him into the house, took me aside and said, 'See what your little temper can do when you let it get out of hand. You could have killed him and you would have to live with that all your life.'

When Jack got over his grogginess mum told him 'That is what happens when you push people too far; he could have split your skull open or even killed you.'

(I don't think we had any more trouble after that, I think it scared the both of us. I don't think you would find a more honest & down to earth person than Jack).

1947 front right - Jack Rae Freshwater Surf Club team.

Box of Chocolates

Dad took us all to the Royal Easter Show in Sydney. We came to a stand where if you could knock over the doll with a wooden ball you won a box of chocolates. I wanted to win a box of chocolates for mum. Cool brother Jack looked at the dolls took aim and knocked one over and won. I got the ball in my hand, looked at the dolls, drew my hand back, head down, and hit the box of chocolates.
After that we had pie and peas for lunch in the big Marquee Tent. It had long trestles for tables and stools to sit on.

There used to be a dairy behind us. Sometimes we would go over and watch them milk the cows. There was also a stone house and piggery on Harbord Rd. where I would go sometimes and watch the farmer feed the pigs. A high school has been built there now. Just below the piggery, was a Chinese Market Garden, where some of my mates and I managed to steal a watermelon without getting caught.

Mum & Dad

When I was growing up mum was always there and we felt secure. The washing was done in the copper. She hand wrung them, then starched the clothes before hanging them on the clothesline; when they were dry she ironed them.
Down on her hands and knees mum used to scrub and polish floors once a week, as well as the old kitchen table. The only carpet we had then was a runner, from the front door to the kitchen.
Dad worked five and half days a week, and when he arrived home about 1 pm on Saturdays he'd have his lunch, do any chores that needed doing mow the lawn, do a bit of gardening, have a wash and then go down the local pub. He'd have his two or three middies a smoke and a yarn with his mates, and then back home for dinner. Mum and her friends would call on one another, and have a chinwag over a cup of tea.

On Sundays dad would do a bit more gardening, or make something to help mother. Yet as busy as they were, they could still find time to take us children on family picnics, and outings. There were no takeaway dinners or frozen foods in those days. Mum used to get up first in the morning, cut our lunches, and make sure we all had a cooked breakfast when we were going to work. Yet with all mum had to do, she was always there to listen to our troubles and attend to our bumps and bruises.

Dad was always there to back mum up, but it was hard for a man to really get to know the children. Having to go to work he wasn't always able to be there when he was needed.

It was hard for this reason, for a man to rear children on his own, particularly girls, as I was to find out later in life

For this reason, I grew up believing that women were the backbone of the country, and therefore had to be respected and protected.

Therefore no man or boy sat while a girl or lady was standing. For the same reason, you did not see elderly people stand; they had done their part and deserved that respect.

I WAS BORN IN TOONGABBIE

THE DEPRESSION

In the depression, people visited one another more often; families organized family outings and every one joined in the activities. I believe some of the wealthier people used to have wine with their meals as this at the time seemed the socially accepted thing to do, although I don't think they all did.

Eggs and chops were fried in fat; the roast dinner was cooked in heaps of fat along with the baked potatoes and pumpkin. Fish and chips were cooked in fat; if you brought a bottle of milk to drink it had about 1 inch of cream on top.

While we were living on the hill, my father got relief work; that meant he worked for a fortnight and had a fortnight off. I believe this came about because my mother went to Manly Police Station and told them that my father had left home, and that she was going to leave the kids the next day. They asked where my father was mum said: She didn't know and did not care, as he had no work and couldn't keep them.

The next day the Police arrived and asked my mother if they got my father relief work could she get in touch with him. When my mother said yes, they told her that he was to report to the Harbord Quarry. When the Police left, my father came out of the wardrobe where he was hiding.

The Quarry if I remember correctly was in Brighton Street, near where we lived. I remember going over to the Quarry to watch my father work. He was drilling for blasting. In those days they had what we used to call a jump bar about six to seven feet long hexagonal in shape; they used to lift it up, and drop it down turning it at the same time and pour water into the hole, to soften the sand stone. Every now and then they would take the bar out of the hole and put what appeared to be a round washer attached to a peace of wire down the hole and bring out the slurry.

When the hole was three to four feet deep, they would put the gelignite down the hole attached to a detonator and fuse. Light the fuse, and blast the sandstone from the side of the hill. From there he worked on Harbord Football field. This was done by pick and shovel and mattock. There were also mine trolleys on rails. One team would loosen the soil the other would load up the trolleys, then take them down to the lower end tip out the contents, and another gang would level it out.

War Time

When the second War came my father joined the Civil Construction Corps, I don't know all the places he worked at. The one I remember was the emergency airstrip that was being built near Pit Town NSW. He had taken me there for a week in the dying stages of construction. The sleeping quarters and the mess were made of unlined galvanized iron. The cooler safe where they kept the meat and butter was of a timber frame construction with hessian around the sides. Water was trickled from the top onto the hessian to keep it wet; it was quite cool inside.

I would occasionally ride into Windsor with the water truck. Once dad borrowed two push-bikes and we went for a ride. All I can remember is the bakery, bush land, and the farms. After the war my father worked for the local Council.

When my father started relief work we moved from the hill to a semi-detached house in Evans Street then we moved to Johnson Street, where we lived at the back of people by the name of Mr. & Mrs. McElaine. Their house faced Harbord Road. They had a garage at the back of their house where they repaired motor vehicles.

 Mr. McElaine used to train men to box of an evening and weekends, and I would hang around. At times they would find me something to do in the garage, like doing a valve grind which made me feel important.

Then we moved to Albert Street, into a semi-detached house where we lived next door to people by the name of Hall. Mr. Hall worked for the Manly Steam Ship Company. They had one son Roy, and three daughters Doreen, Betty, & Pat (flowered pants) and his wife's name was Pearl.

The house had four rooms, two bedrooms, lounge, kitchen and the bathroom was at one end of the back verandah of the weather board house. It had both a front and back verandah where we boys slept. My father was still on relief work. I remember the gas meter-man calling. In those days the gas meter was under the kitchen sink. You had to put 1 shilling into the meter every time you ran out of gas. However you could disconnect the pipes on both sides of the meter, pull an inner tube of a pushbike over both ends of the pipe by-passing the meter and get free gas. When the meter man knocked at the door and called out 'Gasman!',

Mother thought quickly and said, 'I have a cake in the oven! Could you go next door first? It only has a few minutes to go!' when he agreed my mother sent me down to the tool shed to get the 'Stillson's' so she could connect up the meter again.

I think the meter man knew what we were up to; you could see all the marks on the connecting bolts. (Money was hard to come by in those days).

To get a bath we had to boil the water in the old wood-burning copper, and carry it inside to the bath. Through the week we had a birdbath, as we called them, in a dish.

I remember the milkman coming around one morning to collect his money. Mum & Dad were still in bed, when I told them. Mum said, 'I haven't got the money to pay him.' Who's going to tell him?

I said, 'I would' when I told him that it was Dad's fortnight off.

He said, 'It's a pity your old man worked at all'.

I said, 'Yes, then you wouldn't get your money at all'. Later on the families were around the table laughing about what I had said. At the time I could not understand why they were laughing as all I did was tell the truth.

William & Eileen Rae

COUPONS

When the war came as far as I was concerned we were in clover. Dad and Alf had full time work. We had fresh fruit and vegetable every day, clothes out of the shop (as many as our ration coupons would allow) and we could go to the barbers for a haircut. We used to get sixpence to go to the movies on Saturday afternoon and a penny to spend or three pence if we stayed home. We had our own chook's and a vegetable garden.

COUSIN BULLA

I had another auntie and uncle living not far from us named Williams. Mum and Dad went away for a few days, the first holiday they had since they were married. The rest of the family was all working by this time except me. I was the youngest. My job was to look after the house, so for company I used to invite my cousin Bulla (Leonard) over for lunch each day. The day before mum and dad were due to come home Bulla didn't come to lunch, so I went over to see if he was coming. Aunt Myrtle said, 'If he goes I would have to take the rest of the kids'. I didn't know what to say so I said, Alright' so I had Bulla, Donald, Beryl and Myrtle. So while I' m trying to scratch up a meal while there all sitting around the table, who should walk in but Mum and Dad. They had come home one day early.
I told mum how they all came to be there, so she knocked up some sandwiches and sent them on their way.
Next thing I know Auntie Myrtle was at the side fence telling Mum how she did not know that they were all at our place having lunch. I was supposed to have just asked them over when I told Mum that Auntie did say I

had to take the lot, all Mum said was... I know and she knows I know.

I guess Auntie was getting square, for the time I saw her bed sheets on the clothes line and her kids held them tight while I drove the pegs through the edge of the sheet and into the ground to form a tent. (It made a good tent too).

My Brother Bill

Outbreaks of polio usually occurred in summer, terrifying communities.

Swimming pools, theatres and cinemas were closed during epidemics and large gatherings were shunned. Polio seemed to attack the healthiest and fittest of children and young adults. My brother Bill caught Poliomyelitis when he was about 15 years old, and we had to stay home from school. (I think for about three weeks.) I was 9 years old then. This was the only part I thought was good about it.

The doctor told mum that the best she could hope for was that he might be able to use a wheelchair. Mum had heard about Sister Kenny, so she had him transferred from Manly to Royal North Shore Hospital, where Sister Kenny had a Clinic.

I WAS BORN IN TOONGABBIE

I cannot recall how long Bill was in hospital. I think it was around 2 years; his spine was curved and one of his legs was wasted, but he came out walking without the help of crutches or any another support.

Mum used to travel from Harbord to North Shore to visit him, sometimes three and four times a week. He eventually walked out of hospital, and was employed as an apprentice to an Orthopedic Appliance Maker at either Prince Henry or Prince Alfred Hospital I'm not sure which. He eventually finished up working at Launceston General Hospital in Tasmania.

Bill was a man that never gave up. When he came out of Hospital he taught himself to surf, dance, play tennis and cricket. Anything he took on he gave 100%. Yet for all his battles to overcome the Polio, to be able to compete with the next man he never lost his friendly smile, and was always ready to give a helping hand to others along the way.

I remember when he was 18 he was called up by the Army. He came home as proud as punch, he had passed the medical and been accepted.

Mum didn't say anything to him; she just asked "who the doctor was".

As it turned out, it was our family doctor; Mum went down and gave him a piece of her mind.

When she had finished and calmed down the doctor said that he was so impressed by him, 'How I could tell a boy like your son that he didn't pass, and that he was not wanted and break his spirit I marked his card never to be called". And he never was.

Bill was 65 when he died of a heart attack; I guess the old body could not stand the strain any more.

1937 Bill Rae

I was born in Toongabbie

1943 Bill Rae

I was born in Toongabbie

Subs in the Sydney Harbour

I was about 12 when the Jap subs entered Sydney Harbour. Some of us got our pennies together, and we went across the Harbour on the Manly Ferry, our eyes scanning the harbor waters trying to spot the periscope of the sub that they never found. We used to discuss how, if we saw the "sub" that we could tie something around the periscope so they could not see were they going. (Smiling now; just as well we didn't see that Jap sub, it wouldn't have a chance).
A bloke called Okey Fitton who had a General Store in Harbord, was the Air Raid Warden. He recruited us kids with pushbikes, to carry messages in case of an air raid.
I asked mum if it would be all right; she said, 'Yes'.
So off I went to the training session, carrying messages around Harbord in the night without lights. When I told mum we all had to assemble at Okey's place if an Air Raid came; and was it still all right, mum said, 'Yes'.
Just as well we didn't have an Air Raid, because otherwise I would have had to use an excuse for why I didn't turn-up that mother and I had a fight, and she had gone back on her word. Frankly I would have been afraid, and if they came looking for me they would have found me under the bed hanging onto mum.
To go for a swim we had to go through a course of zigzag barbwire, to get to the surf. The gates were closed, when

the Army had target practice, and no one was allowed on the beach.

Movie Theatres

In the early days, there used to be a Movie Theatre at Queenscliff where the seats were deck chairs placed in rows across the Theatre. After a Cowboy Movie was shown, the seats were no longer in a line, because the kids used to ride them around. The Theatre was closed down for a time, and when it re-opened the seats were made of flash leather. If I remember correctly, the movie that was shown when it re-opened was called "Show Boat" starring Paul Robeson, an African-American singer and actor. I remember in the movie, him sitting on a chair shelling peas singing "Ah Still Suits Me" (I still suit me) and the peas rolling down a paper funnel into the pea bowl. Another movie I watched there was "Tall Timbers", a 1937 action film, set in the timber industry and directed by Ken G. Hall. The foyer was decorated with gum tree branches; it cost sixpence down stairs and nine-pence upstairs. It must have been about the time I used to help the fruit and vegetable man on Saturday mornings, because I always had two-shillings to spend at interval. I used to buy 3 or 4 Ice cream buckets @ three-pence each, and tip the ice-cream-boy.

Naturally I got quick service, and I would then give the other 2 or 3 buckets away when I saw someone who didn't have money to spend' Big Time Charlie!

There was another Movie Theatre in Manly almost opposite the Amusement Pier near the Ferry wharf. It was called 'The Embassy' (I believe the name had changed some years ago). Before the main feature started, the management would put on a sing-along with the bouncing-ball bouncing above the words on the screen. When the song finished a man would move to centre stage and say 'All together now, North, South, East and West, Embassy Matinees are the best'. Jimmy Clark and I went there one Saturday afternoon; there must have been a Cowboy Movie on, because we were both stamping our feet. When Jim stopped stamping, and said, 'I felt something warm on my leg' he looked around, and said, 'You dirty little bugger'.

When I looked behind him, there was a little boy down on his knees, with both hands on the back of Jim's seat. He was nearly in tears, saying, 'I couldn't wait' naturally all I could do was laugh. It didn't happen to me.

I WAS BORN IN TOONGABBIE

When us kids started wanting things, another song mum sang to us in a slightly irritating way, was a short version of –

♪ Little lady make believe Lyrics ♪
by Eddy Arnold

Dream your little dreams and may they all come true
May the coming years bring happiness to you
Dream your little dreams and may they come true
May the coming years bring happiness to

Myers Bakery Oct 1942

At the age of 13 ½, I started work on the Bread Cart at Myers Bakery for Bert Myers He was a cranky old bugger.
Every day before he started work they would bring him out his raw egg and milk to drink for his ulcer. Then he used to turn round, and put his legs apart so he could squat down a bit to break wind.

He and I never used to get on too well.

I got on well with his daughter, Heather Norsan. She was married to a bloke in the Airforce at the time, and their son Jack Myers was in the Airforce.

We used to do the Harbord run, and sometimes we'd do the Queenscliff run.

One day Bert and I had a bitter dispute.

Bert said, 'Short-changed - we're short of money - it doesn't add up'.

Heather Norsan uses to do all the adding up of the books.

He said,' We are a few bob short here and there, you must have got it wrong', and they blamed me.

I said, ' I didn't'.

They said, 'It was you, you did it' and I said, 'No I didn't'.

They said, 'You did it and don't be stupid'.

So, one day we were out in the Cart and we'd just come to our first Customer, he got in the back of the cart and he found 2/- (two shillings).

And he said, 'There, you don't care about my money you just drop it and losing it here and there'.

All right then, I said, 'I'll count mine and you count yours' and I counted mine and mine was right; he found a hole in his bag. It was him that was dropping the money. So that we could sort it out, as far as the shortages go, Heather gave me a receipt book and I wrote out a receipt when any one paid a bill.

So we went around and we marked it all off, and I found out I was right! My money was always right, his wasn't.
He used to go down to the pub and have a few beers after work and forget how many paid him down there. That was one fight we had.
Another time we were out the back of the cart and I dropped a loaf of bread, and he started dancing around me in circles yelling abuse with his fists, going up and down. He just kept following me around all day, going crook about me dropping his bread; yelling at me, 'Didn't I care about his bread...
'Don't you care about my bread'...going on and on and in the end I yelled at him, 'No!, and that finished that argument.

A Horse named Peter

The horse Peter was a big roan. He was a quiet country horse standing 17 hands high and he wasn't used to the noisy city life. He used to start, and was a very nervous horse.
Bert couldn't handle him too well, and he used to treat him roughly.
I had to take him down the blacksmith's one time to Danny Inskip's in Manly, so I took him down and I

talked to the horse while he shoed him and we had no trouble.

After that anytime he needed to be shod Bert got me to take him down because I could talk to the horse and got along with him and we never had any trouble - I loved that horse.

Peter trusted me, and I would do anything for him, and he would do anything for me.

One day I was at the back of the cart getting bread out and Bert was up ahead doing a few places and I had done mine and come back to get more bread to go up the other side.

And Bert whistles Peter, and Peter was having a feed the sharp whistle and the yell startled him and Peter took off.

The top of the door hit me on the back of the head, flattened me out and sent the bread flying! Later they found Peter round at Curl Curl Beach near the Clubhouse.

The paper man was doing the rounds delivering papers. He was in his car, he pulled over and he held him up until I came for Peter and the Cart so we could finish the run. (Bert never could handle the flamin horses)

Peter Spencer took him out once, he said he was going to fix him, and I didn't know what he was going to do. When he bought him back you could see where all the skin was worn off where the collar was too small and tight; he must have given him hell I think.

Uphill and down dale I was as mad as a wet hen, but I couldn't do anything about it.

No one could get near Peter after that for a long time, but I could still go over to him. He remembered me, I'd give him a feed and talk to him.

Horses are terrific once you get to know them, and are not frightened of them.

DOLLY

When I knocked off one of the runs they asked me to go around and pick up a horse. She was a dark black mule-eared old horse and she was as grumpy as Bert was.

Well that was a spare horse, in-case the others were being shod then she used to pull the cart around.

They left her in a paddock at Johnston Street; it had a big paling fence around it.

When we came in Cathy Newson came out and said to me, 'Look, the boys said they were going to bring Dolly down'.

She said, 'They have been away a long time, could you go up there and have a look'.

So I walked up to Johnson Street, (it was right next door were my brother Alf had built his house) and there's the kids sitting on the fence with winkers and reins.

 I said, 'what's up, are you going to catch it?'

They said, 'You can't catch it, it goes you.'
So I got the winkers rolled up in one hand and the reins in the other; and I started walking up to her.
She came at me head straight out and showing her teeth, so I've got the winkers across my body and I thought I am going to knock your head one way and I am going the other way. As she came right up close and I was about to strike when she stopped, and she stuck her head down.
She was bluffing, so I put the reins on her, and I brought her home.

Busy Times

Sometimes the bakers would ask me to go in at 12 O'clock on a Sunday night and give them a hand. I would go to our younger set club at the Local Institute, dance till 11 O'clock, run home, get changed and up to the bakery by 12 O'clock. Come home at 6 O'clock change again muck up the bed so mum wouldn't know I had not slept in it then back out again to do the bread deliveries.
In later years I have thought back about the Myers. They were a nice family; I often wonder how they tolerated me. (Maybe bread carters were hard to come by)

I was born in Toongabbie

The Black Smiths

I finished up giving the bread carting away for a while, and worked for Danny Inskip the Blacksmith. My job was shoeing horses, as well as going out and bringing the horses in to be shod, and taking them back home again. Of course I got a couple of extra bob a week for that.

I was too short for anvil work, and I needed a box to stand on. Sometimes when he would get cranky, I would occasional turn the crank handle the wrong way and it would wrench his fist.

The blacksmith was about a 26 minute walk from home. Starting at Albert Street, I turn left onto Lawrence St, another left onto Oliver St, turn left again onto Pittwater road, then onto Balgowlah Road, go past the Tramway Depot, then walk down Kenneth road, between Manly Golf Course and the park.

Past the Ice Works, take the track beside a house,(near Graham Reserve), before arriving at The Blacksmith.

I had never ridden a horse before; it was my job to ride out on a quiet pony leave it and ride the other horse to the blacksmiths. Some of them were not very quiet I never had a saddle, I was told I had to toughen my rear end up first I lost some skin and I would ride almost along the horse's neck. I always straightened up leaving and coming towards the blacksmith shop; eventually my rear end healed and I was given a saddle. I guess I rode every type of horse from a pony to a draught horse.

A Cow of a Horse

One day we had this horse named Dolly to shoe. She was a cow horse, she would kick and squeal and wet everywhere. You had to put a rope around her neck and tie her up onto a hook on a pole, then another rope went over her body and had her leg that was being shod held up high.

I had to hold it out with the hook to get the old shoes off. She finished up losing her footing and lying down on the ground, head up in the air and breathing hard.

I said, 'Get her up'.

He said, 'Let the bitch lay there - she'll get up', I couldn't see how she was going to do it on 3 legs, but she got up herself. It took the two of us to shoe her and we had to rope up each leg in turn to get that job done.

Then the paper shop had another mule eared small horse I got that damned thing shod. I was riding her home one night to the paper shop in Harbord, when we hit the bitumen road with its new shoes.

I was starting to pull her up, and make her slow down; because just past there, was a tram depot, on Pitt Water Road; there were 2 sets of tramlines and they were down low, and where they had tarred the road and it had bulges everywhere.

I was going along and I had no saddle; when both the horse's feet went outside ways head went down and I went over the top.

She got up first, shot straight over the top of me & put one foot on my chest and moved me and took the skin off my back.

I got up chasing the horse trying to catch it. Just then Danny Inskip was coming along in his sulky with his trotter, and he was having a bit of a laugh.

When I got up there he said, 'What happened, did you fall off?'

I said, 'Yea' (Danny had a bad habit of stating the obvious and always with that same silly grin on his face.)

Any way I caught the horse and rode home that day.

The Pony

After working for Danny Inskip for a while he gave me a pony to ride to and from work. Her name was One Eye. I use to ride her home to Albert Street and tie her up by the fence, and give her a feed she could pick around and get some grass, and then I could ride her into work in the morning.

Any way one day I was feeling a bit tired, so I put her nose for home and I just let her go, laid on the saddle closed the eyes and had a snooze. I knew what she was doing and I trusted her and she trusted me.
She took me along and when I got to the side of the fence, were I tied her up she whinnied and woke me up; and when I woke up there's Kath Newson, and the women from the paper shop. And another woman down the fence out on the footpath looking down to me called 'Are you alright, are you alright?', I said 'Yea, I was just tired and went to sleep and she brought me home.
 We thought something might have happened to you, and they were all worried.
I said, ' No, I am all right' and I tied her up I could trust her with my life. She knew that she didn't get ill-treated from me either she was an old horse;
The boys were sent to bring in a pony at Balgowlah. When I arrived the guys were sitting on the fence.
 I said, 'What's up? They said, 'Well we can't catch it'
 So I got the bridle and reins and I went in, and it runs into the corner, with its head in the corner of the fence lashing out with its back legs.
 I remembered something Mum told me a long time ago, that if you are having trouble, get a long stick and you put it on their back, and you then move in on the horse as you slowly and gently move the stick up their back.
When it's on their back and they don't know what it is, they stay very still.

So this is what I did, and I got right up to its head I couldn't get its ear, I got its mane, and when I did get its mane, and with the other arm around its neck it reared up in the air, and me with it hanging on.

When its feet came down and I touched the ground I grabbed its ear and held onto that, and it couldn't do anything while I had his ear because it was hurting.

I got the bridle and I shoved it on him and I let the boys take him back, because I had to get another horse.

When I got back Danny Inskip, said, 'They told me you couldn't catch him'.

Laughingly I said, 'The rotten liars! I hated liars'.

Pommies

I used to pick some horses up from the Dairy at Balgowlah, and he always called me a Pommy, (they teased you; Pommies wouldn't know anything about horse) I got a bit narked at being called a Pommy. I took the horse back and I said to something to Danny. "Ah he hates Pommies himself.

He's got a Pommy working for him; the girl up there is a Pommy.

Just tell him any more of this Pommy business and tell him to step outside and have it out. 'Well I was about this high and he was that high and he called me a Pommy and I walked up and said, "Step outside and we will settle it." We never had any more arguments or

Pommy after that. Gore, I could have got into trouble for that.

Another time I went out to get the horse from Balgowlah and I had to pick it up once it came in from its run. (As far as the horse figured it had finished its work and wasn't leaving the yard.)

And it wasn't going to go, a big bay, so I got it out in the yard and they started hitting it with the broom. They broke the straw broom on its behind, but it still wouldn't go.

And she kept bucking every time they did it, and that is all it would do, so I had to turn it around, backed it right down to the end of the street and round the corner, then I turned it around and headed into the direction I needed her to go.

When it couldn't see the bakery it was alright after that, and thought it better go along and get its shoes done.

Wild Ride

Behind the Council Chambers there was a Bakery. They had a big bay carthorse in the stables, and every time I tried to get into the stables trying to get near its head, it was quicker than me and it would turn around quickly; it was very supple.

If I wasn't careful he would get me in the back of the stalls and then if he raced up the side and spins I would be crushed.

I tried going across the top again and it finished up that I couldn't get him.

A bloke that knew him and drove him every day, would have to come in and get him for me, and pull him out. I would take him home, then next day I'd take him into the blacksmith and get him shod.

When I was taking the shoes off the horse, he had his back leg up and over me. I thought Oh he's peaceful, this is easy. He was relaxed and I relaxed. Then a fly must have got on him and annoyed him because the foot I was hanging onto flew up in the air. I went through the air and landed on my bum & skidded along through the dust.

Danny Inskip laughed and said, 'Did he send you flying, did he?'

After he was shod we came out and I went to take him back to Manly,

He got onto the tarred road and he knew he was going home and he took off.

He was on the tarred road with new shoes, he had a hard mouth, and if I'd tried to saw his mouth to hold him he might have slipped and we both would have come down, so all I could do was hang-on and hold his head tight as much as I could. I was riding bare back; I had no saddle so I couldn't stand up on the stirrups and make him sit down on his back legs. I just had to sit there and hold tight. The big bay horse galloped through and across Pitt Water Road. We went across that ok and down to a back street.

On the right was the old road to Sydney. We went straight across that and behind the Post Office, and that's where a lot of traffic's going both ways all the time and I couldn't pull him up. I thought 'I hope to hell there's no car's coming,' and that's all I could do.

When he got down the end it was on a very sharp dogleg turn that backed up a laneway behind Coles and Woolworth's. Lucky for me the horse slowed down and walked the rest of the way home.

BACK TO THE BAKERY

Around 13 ½ nearly 14 years of age, I went back to the Bakery then again for awhile, because they offered me more money.

A couple of times I had to do the runs on my own because one of the bread carters was off sick and the other one was an ex-serviceman back from the war; he had something wrong with him and had to go to the ex-serviceman's Hospital sometimes.

I had to take his cart out and do the run; I got half a day and then when he got back he helped me with the other half.

I was born in Toongabbie

Carthorse named Dolly

We had a carthorse there called Dolly, and she used to lash out with her back leg whenever you went to the back of the cart and stood on the back step. If you weren't watching or ready for her, she would get you.

She used to hurt her own leg as well on the back step, and had a sore from hitting the iron step.

Anyway; Bert turned around up at Queenscliff, backed up and the wheels went down a ditch off the edge of the road, because we were facing across the road.

As she tried to pull up he tried to get her to pull out, and she couldn't because her steel hoofs kept slipping and she would go down on her front knees.

She went down the second time and as she got up we could see she had taken the skin off, and he turned around and lashed out at her to get her going again.

When she fell again, I got down off the cart and held her head down.

Bert said, 'What will I do?'

I said, 'Let go of the reins and release the traces'.

When he got down and released the traces and I let her up I took her over and tied her to a lamp-post.

Right, I said, 'Now you get in the shafts, and you pull and I'll get on the wheel and I'll turn it'.

So he got in the shafts and I turned the wheel where the bump was and it lifted up and came out.

Bert said, 'Now, I could have done that in the first place'. Why didn't you think of that before?'

I said, 'I don't know'.

But I got a lot of satisfaction in seeing old Bert in those shafts pulling that cart and I wasn't allowed to live it down for a long time.

Transport

In those days the 'Toastrack Trams' were the main transport in Sydney, with their running board or step along the full length of the tram. In peak hour the Trams used to be banked up from Circular Quay to the Town Hall. The smoking carriages were at each end of the tram and had a canvas blind you could pull down in wet weather; the non-smoking section had sliding doors. To catch the early ferry to Manly, some of us every time the tram stopped would hop off the one we were on, and run down the side of the trams, then hop on one, three or four trams ahead. We would keep this up till we reached the Quay. If you kept an eye on the conductor you could miss out on paying your fare.

In those times the Manly Ferries were crowded, and you would be lucky if you could get a seat on the stairs leading to the upper deck. When the ferry approached the boom gates there was a net stretched across the harbour to prevent submarines entering. The lights would be turned off till it had proceeded well past the

I was born in Toongabbie

heads to Sydney Harbour, then the lights would come on again.

If you wanted to be one of the first off, you would take up an early position on the leeward side where the gangplanks were tied into place. Some of the more adventurous would stand on the rail and jump onto the wharf; a few would slip on the decking of the wharf in wet weather and land on their rear ends including yours truly, but only once.

I remember one person dressed in his suit and hat, his arms wrapped around two potted palms and a brief case in his hand. He was trying to walk up the outside of the gangplank hanging onto the rail; he slipped and went into the water. I looked down and all I could see was two palms rising out of the water with a bald head in the middle. When the deck hand pulled him out, he did look a miserable sight. But he still had his two pot plants and brief case, I never did find out what happened to his hat.

If, when you arrived at the bus pick up area and were not at least half way along the queue, you would have to wait fifteen to twenty minutes for the next bus to Harbord.

The buses at that time had all the glass windows taken out and metal windows were installed except for the driver's window.

The buses were painted in a camouflage pattern, and all the lights were dimmed. Headlights were fitted with downward reflection bars.

We would knock off work at 4:30pm and arrive home about 6:15pm.

14 Year's Old

I reached the legal age to work which if I remember correctly was 14 years and 3 months. The war was on so you had to report to The Commonwealth Employment Service and they let you go to the job. You were issued with an identity card which you were supposed to carry with you at all times.

I went tent making in Castlereagh Street. We were making Signal Flags for the Navy, also tents for the Army, and tents for the Army Hospital. At that stage I had not been working at the tent place for long when an opportunity came for me to be an apprentice painter with the Port Jackson & Manly Steamship Co.

In those days you had to get permission to change your place of employment. The War was still on, and The Employment Service had to direct the labour where it was most needed.

So mum and I went off to the Employment Office in Sydney and after a short conversation, and a phone call to my employer and an assurance that the

C.E.S could replace me; I was allowed to start my apprenticeship with the Port Jackson and Manly Steamship Co.

I WAS BORN IN TOONGABBIE

Apprenticeship

I started my apprenticeship as a painter at the Port Jackson and Mainly Steam Ship Co. I found painting dull; when I first started I was mixing paints, cleaning brushes, burning out paint tins and 44-gallon drums then scraping the old paint out of them.
One day I was scraping out one of the 44-Gallon Drums (you burn them out and then brush the rust off). I was leaning over cleaning this drum getting the rust off, and someone had found half a rock melon floating in the harbour and let me have it fair in the back of the skull.
 It damn near sent me into the drum. When I looked around there was not a soul to be seen anywhere. I set off to find out who it was and I was going to take him on; just as well I didn't find out that day. I got the seeds out of my head and finished the job I was doing.
It was weeks later before I found out who did it. They said, 'We were hiding down behind the board,'
 I said, 'Yes I was that mad I would have come after you too' (by the time I found who had done it, I had cooled down and could see the humour of it).
Apprenticeships did not pay much for the first year you received enough to pay your fares to work and go to a movie or a dance.

I was born in Toongabbie

Mum and dad still had to keep me, and I would go to tech school at night, things improved a little when I started painting with undercoat, then onto actual painting and varnishing.

Another time, I was lying down on the upper deck, on my own, painting in-between the length of the seats in the middle. I was so bored and uninterested; to break the monotony I started to sing.

♫ *I don't want to set the world on fire* ♫

I just want to start
A flame in your heart
In my heart I have but one desire
And that one is you
No other will do

I've lost all ambition for worldly acclaim
I just want to be the one you love
And with your admission that you feel the same
I'll have reached the goal I'm dreaming of

Believe me!
I don't want to set the world on fire
I just want to start
A flame in your heart

I WAS BORN IN **TOONGABBIE**

Horace Heidt

- words and music by Eddie Seiler, Sol Marcus, Bennie Benjamin and Eddie Durham

♪

Next thing I heard a voice, which laughingly sang out from down below saying, 'Don't worry mate you won't'.

There was a painter there that belonged to the Salvation Army. Whenever I was working with him and he looked tired or down in the dumps I would sing...

♫ ***John Brown's Body Lies A-Mouldering in the Grave*** ♫

John Brown's body lies a-mouldering in the grave,
John Brown's body lies a-mouldering in the grave,
But his soul goes marching on.
Chorus:
Glory, glory, hallelujah, / |
Glory, glory, hallelujah,
His soul goes marching on.

He's gone to be a soldier in the Army of the Lord, / |
He's gone to be a soldier in the Army of the Lord,
His soul goes marching on.
Chorus:

I was born in Toongabbie

John Brown's knapsack is strapped upon his back, /
John Brown's knapsack is strapped upon his back,
His soul goes marching on.
Chorus:

John Brown died that the slaves might be free, /
John Brown died that the slaves might be free,
His soul goes marching on.
Chorus:

The stars above in Heaven now are looking kindly down, /
The stars above in Heaven now are looking kindly down,
His soul goes marching on.

~

You would see a grin come on his face and he would usually say 'Good on you brother.' (To see that big smile made my day).

I think what made me decide to finish with painting, was the time Percy the Boss sent me down underneath the forecastle (fo'c'sle) the forward part of a ship, the sailors' living quarters, to touch up were the previous painter had chipped and red-leaded. I was told 'There's a job that will take you all day. There's another painter down there and it's touching up'. When we arrived all I could see was three bolt heads to do and there were already about 10 men working. He didn't have anymore work for us, so my mate slept the first half, and I slept the second half, then we came and touched up and returned the paint to the paint shop, cleaned our brushes and paint tins, then headed off for home.

Another time I got into some trouble; was because I was told to chip all the rust off and to red lead all the side of the boat. I went round and I had that finished before the day was up.

Someone said, 'You're a Bloody Hero aren't you'.

I said, 'No – why, all I did was get the job finished'.

I was very active and I liked to get things done, and the way they were going it was just too slow for me so I ended up throwing it in.

I was going to tech for sign writing and after 12 months, and I had had enough of the mates, I was hanging around with. So I went and did some work on the Pontoon at Manly.

Manly Pool Pavilion

The Manly Pool had entertaining pontoons, slides and treadmills. Crowds flocked to the pool, boardwalk, and fun-pier. On one of the wheels you get on and run with it, and if you can't keep up with the wheel as it gets faster, you finish up in the water again.

It had a big walkway across to the other side; the top walkway for walkers, and the lower walkway for the swimmers. What we had to do was paint it, and as you painted it you threw sand on it. My job was to keep throwing the sand on it, and that made it non-slippery for the people to walk on.

And that was an interesting job - it was close to home and a change from working in the dockyard.

Day Dreams

In 1944, I had ideas of going to the country becoming a roustabout in the shearing sheds and learning droving, in the off seasons. There were tales going around at the time about how the drovers and shearers would go into town, and blow their cheques at the local pub, and get into fights. Mum wasn't going to stop me even though I was only 15 at the time. I could see mum was worried so I knocked that idea on the head.

The Younger Set

I joined the Younger Set, which held meetings at the Harbour Institute on Sunday nights; I think the age limit was from 15 to 20 years of age. Two adults were present. One played the piano, the other supervised; we made all our own decisions as to outings and the way money was raised through fees and raffles and how it was spent.

After the meetings we would hold a dance till 11pm. I did not have a clue how to dance and was not real interested until three or four of the local girls dragged me onto the floor to do the barn dance.

(I wonder if it was because I had lost my freckles and my hair stayed combed, that changed their attitude towards dancing with me).

After this they taught me a few other dances. From then on I decided to learn ballroom dancing.

Not long after I joined the Younger Set, the 'Jitterbug' came into vogue.

A girl by the name of Colleen decided to teach me how it was done. While holding my hand she spun me away then pulled me back towards her. By this time I had lost control of my feet on the slippery floor. As I was propelled back towards her she threw out her chest, and I finished up sitting on the floor.

I was invited to an Engagement party held at the Institute and the presents were placed on a card table against the wall. We were all dancing to records when someone put on the song Hokey Pokey; when it came to the part were the group you were dancing with held hands and went around in a circle, the group would put the pace on and at a pre-arranged signal they would let someone's hands go. And the chosen one would go sliding across the floor. This time it was yours truly's turn, and there I was sliding across the floor on my stomach heading straight for the card table with the presents on it.

How I managed to pass under the table without touching the legs and finish up with my feet against the wall I do not know. I could see myself working for 12 months to replace the presents.

The Younger Set had an outing to Narrabeen Lakes. We rowed up the lake to Middle Creek, all bush land then with a clear waterfall. I remember activities were slowing down. So I decided I would have a swim, when I noticed one of the groups had decided to take one of the boats out for a row (as I had said, nearly everyone was having a rest before rowing back to the boat shed about 6 km away).

So I swam across the creek until I was in-line with the boat under the water.

I put my hands out in front of me to grab the front of the boat then worked my way under the boat and came up at the stern. I heard some screams from the shore just before my head went under. When I looked over the stern everyone was chattering and looking over the sides.

I asked if they had lost something then put my head under the water and swam away in case someone got upset.

Rowing home our boat became stuck on a sand bar. We decided who ever pushed us off the sand bar didn't have to row back to the boat shed. The girls hopped over the side and pushed us off. I think they enjoyed it as much as we did. I think I was a bit sour at girls for the way they looked and spoke about me at school but I was slowly changing my opinion. They were starting to look and act differently to what they did back then.

On another outing we used to have we would walk from Harbord to Oxford Falls, a distance of approximately 9km for a Picnic, then afterwards we would walk home, have dinner then change our clothes then go up to the institute and dance till 11pm.

Reg and Joyce's cat

Bill, Jack & Reg Rae

I WAS BORN IN **TOONGABBIE**

I USED TO GO TO DANCES AT MANLY

The dances were held at The Lurna Dance Hall at Dee Why War Memorial Club in Manly and Freshwater Surf Club.
The uniformed Police would drop in every now and then to check that there weren't any troublemakers; no one seemed to mind.
It was after the age limit was dropped from 21 to 18 years of age that the dances seemed to fade out. That meant that sixteen-year-olds could also go to the pubs and clubs. As proof of age was not needed or asked for, the Hotels hired bands to compete with the club for the dollar. The hotels became nosier; the bands became louder until you could hardly hear yourself talk. It was as if they were competing with the drinkers to be heard. Then the bands started to arrive in torn jeans singlet and unshaven. Whether this was a way of drawing attention to themselves I do not know. All I know is they set the fashions and others followed.
There was a Country and Western singer, who made an appearance at the War Memorial Club dance I think her name was Judy Connors. She looked rather attractive in her outfit and I liked the way she yodeled, I thought to myself; I wouldn't mind a dance with her. After she finished singing there were so many big wolves around

her, I reckoned this little cub didn't stand a chance; I stayed loyal to the local girls.

North Manly Football Club

Some of my mates formed the North Manly Football Club. I was nearly 16, the year was 1945, and our home ground was on Pittwater Road near the Balgowlah Golf Course. The grounds had a tin shed with a pan toilet, and the urinal inside it was also used as a change room. In those days you didn't have to produce a birth certificate to play. We had to buy our own football gear and pay 1/- (one shilling) ground fees each time we played; if you wanted to wash the mud off after the game you jumped into the creek which ran alongside the field.

With the running around delivering bread, bike riding, swimming, loading and unloading trucks in the wholesale store and working as a blacksmith striker; I had the physique of an 18-year-old, as a doctor who was to examine me later had said.

Our team lost many games, and unfortunately I did not finish the season. I contracted Poliomyelitis that year.

Sister's Wedding

When Bert Guest returned from the War in the Middle East he married my sister Joyce (her first name was Alice but she always preferred to be called Joyce, ever since I remember). The Reception was held at my Aunt Emily's house at Balgowlah. If you did not have plenty of money receptions were an aus'tere thing in those days. And of course you had to watch your ration Coupons, which limited the number of guests, and you could not get beer for love or a small amount of money.
Later on they had two sons Albert and Derrick known as Beau and Rick. When Bert came home from New Guinea, he had lost his right hand, and had to learn to use Artificial Gadgets.

I was born in Toongabbie

William Rae, Eileen Rae, Joyce Guest, Bert Guest & Ricky Guest

1945

I had only a few days to go before I would reach that magical age of sixteen years when I started to realize, how little my parents knew about life, how people had changed since their day.
Even so they managed to keep the eight of us together through a depression then fed, clothed and educated us with a whole two weeks' salary, which had to stretch to four weeks. Then Dad got full-time-work and was buying the house we lived in. (They did not have a clue how to handle money, thought I, whereas I had just about found a way to solve the World's Problems).
I had left the Pontoon work and started working as a Store-man for Distributors
Of Wholesale Groceries, and I was there for quite some time and getting on well.
That is when I contracted Poliomyelitis.
(I went to Hospital from there, and was unable to pass this knowledge and wisdom onto mum and dad, unlike my own children when they reached that magical age. I was fortunate enough to have them pass this knowledge on to me.)
 I often wonder how much things have really changed, apart from science coming up with things like DDT in the fifties spraying everything we ate, arsenic in cattle dips, which I have heard it is still unsafe to use on the

ground around them, and new and more efficient war weapons.

Lawn mowers burn a mixture of petrol and oil fumes to breathe into your lungs, instead of the light push mower that runs on muscle power.

My recipe for living is eating good plain food, everything else in moderation, live and let live, and if you want respect show respect for others.

Polio

I went to The Prince Henry Coast Hospital, near Botany Bay where it was confirmed that I had Poliomyelitis. I was sent to isolation, in a room on my own laid out in bed on my back. They tied both my arms up at the elbows to the back of the bed. (I felt no pain except when the doctor sent a needle into my spine for the purpose of taking of fluid sample); testing for meningitis, but it was Polio. This was after I had an enema. (This meant I had a tube inserted into my rectum to allow fluid to be poured into my bowel to flush it out; something I did not appreciate).

I had to lie on my back; I couldn't get my hands to meet. I was in the Isolation ward, no one to talk to, no wireless to listen to, and my arms tied to the back of the bed, so I could not read. All I could do was lie there and contemplate my future, which at the time seemed grim (I wished I could finish it there and then).

When these moods came over me I would sing to take my mind off it, then I would think of others I had seen and think about how they managed until my mind focused on people being pushed around in a wheelchair, then the black mood would take over again.

Looking out the window I could only see a brick wall. Nurse Quong came around, a little Chinese nurse, and she said, 'Look at the view'

I said, 'Yes, it's a brick wall;' so she turned my bed around, and held me up so I could have a look and see the Golf Course, and the Coast. She was quite pleasant.

But then I was getting a bit mad about it all, especially when they said I couldn't walk. I said, 'I'm sick of being tied up like this, I want to get out of here'.

The nurse said, 'What for - you couldn't walk anyway - you couldn't even get out of bed'.

I thought, I walked in here, I could walk out.

Somehow I got out of these things they had tied me up in. I'm getting out.

I swung my legs over the bed, and went to sit up, and I couldn't get up.

I'm balancing on the side of the bed; my body was stiff, like a wooden board. It was pulling on the muscles and I was hurting.

After all attempts to get in or out of bed failed it finished up I had to sing out to get help, because I couldn't go forwards and I couldn't go back. I had to call out for help, and for the first time in my life I felt real fear. At that stage no one could tell me whether I would walk, be confined to a wheelchair, or on my back being hand fed, as the nurses were doing then.

MCNAMARA FRAME

Over the next 3 weeks and they had different doctors looking at me, and they decided I was going to be completely immobilized and put me in a McNamara Frame. My legs would be strapped apart, the rest of my body tied up to my chest, my arms tied up in the air. I didn't want this because of my brother Bill and his troubles with it. So I told Mum what they intended to do. I said, 'They want to put me in a McNamara Frame, and I am not going in any bloody frame for it'.
She said, 'I'll see about it' next thing she came back, and said, 'it's alright, I'm getting you shifted to Sister Kenny Clinic at the Royal North Shore Hospital.'
In later years I have thought of the heartaches mum must have gone through with first Bill then me; yet never showing it, always giving us encouragement.

Mum and Dad may not have at times lived up to our expectations, but they never deserted us when times were tough and they were always there when we needed them.

When I arrived at the Royal North Shore Hospital it was heaven.
The Women's ward was on the upper floor called the Dibbs Ward, and the men's ward was on ground level. It was called the Carey Ward.
 My bed was on the open verandah. The Mattresses were stuffed with what felt like coconut fibres, and then placed on a board on the bed. They were very hard but you got used to them.
There were large blinds that were dropped down in wet weather.
Cleanliness inside and out was the order of the day. The nurse came around each day and checked on our bowel motion. If you didn't go you had to take what looked like a Ford Pill; if that didn't work you had to take Castor Oil and orange juice. If you still did not go you were woken up about 4am and given an enema.

The Sister Kenny Treatment

Elizabeth Kenny was a bush-nurse who, with very little formal training, had some success with treatment for polio that included exercises and heat rather than immobilization. America made a film on Sister Kenny she was unhonoured in her own country.

She was 5 ft. 8 in. tall and weighed 154 lbs; very imposing in stature, with a forceful personality, and seemed like a giant to children.

True to mum's word I was not placed in a frame, although there were others in the wards that were. The doctors were treating them; and they were only taken out long enough for the Physiotherapist to give them exercise.

I was wheeled down to the Kenny Clinic each day, bed and all, and returned to the ward each evening. While I was there, they got blanket strips, put them in boiling water took them out with tongs, put them through a hand wringer then wrapped them around the affected parts of the anatomy, which in my case was the right shoulder to the elbow and the right hip to the knee. They kept doing that for a while to loosen up muscles. Normally it would have burned but it didn't because my muscles were too tight to feel anything. Then the sister would bend my joints until it hurt. This went on for about two months until I could feel the heat of the hot packs and my joints could be bent normally with little pain. Then came the best part I would be laid in an extra-large bath where the sister extended my arms sideways and could exercise my body with the help of the hot water. I was then put onto a table for more exercises.

When I told the boys in the ward about the bath both Joe and Kelly transferred to the Kenny Clinic. After some time when I could sit up on my own and after exercises,

I had to sit up at one end of the bath. At the other end there was a hose attached to the cold water tap. The sister would turn on the water and spray the cold water up and down my spine until I turned pink and purple.

When the others didn't hear me scream any more, they came around the screen to have a look and started laughing. (I must have looked like a drowned rat). I was told the reason for the spray was to get the circulation moving. All I knew was, I was damned cold. However, they did lay me back in the bath to warm me up, before they lifted me out.

We had to drink a glass of milk each day; I was lying on a table, which was parallel with the baths, when the milk was handed out. I was looking to my right when I saw a little hand appear around the screen with a glass of milk in I;, then the hand turned over and poured the milk down the sink.

I said, 'What is going on here?'

Little Richard's head came around the screen with a frown on his forehead and one finger to his lips. I don't know if the sister knew; we never squealed on him.

Wheelchair Run

So we started to get to know the girls upstairs. Their ward was up above us, and we used to signal one

another at night, generally it was me by singing; the others piked it. (Chickened or wimped out)
So I used to sing up to them, and they would sing something back down it was quite a competition between us.
 There was a little girl who came round from upstairs; she'd had an operation on one of her legs because it was shorter, and they operated on the muscle and bone of the leg to lengthen it. She was in plaster when she dropped down to see us. Everybody was signing the plaster cast on her leg, so I signed it as well. We got talking so I got to know her well. They had cottages which they used to send the people over to convalesce before they went home. They stayed until they could get used to walking round, after they had the plaster off and got the muscles working.

One night back in the ward Joe suggested that we each get a wheelchair and go over and visit someone he knew in the cottages. Joe had two dropped feet, so he had no trouble manipulating the wheelchair with his arms. It was a different story for me with one good arm, on one side and only one good hand on the other. I was very slow; still I was willing to give it a go.
 So off we went out through the ward, turned left down a slight slope, turned left again along past the ward, and before I had gone ten-paces, Joe was out of sight. The next time I saw Joe he was coming back in a hurry; as

he passed me he said, 'Quick, I nearly knocked the Matron and the Superintendent over.'

I went back along the path, but then I was in trouble as there was no way I could get that damn chair to go up that incline. Fortunately for me there was a couple waiting outside the opposite ward and the gentleman offered to give me a hand, which I accepted.

When I arrived at the ward, the nurse hurried to wheel me to my bed, and then returned both wheelchairs to their proper place. She then sat at her desk just in time. The Matron and Supervisor came to inspect the ward; naturally all the patients were asleep and the number of wheelchairs allotted to the ward was accounted for.

THE CHALLENGE

Our Favorite song back at the ward was
♪ ***I'll be home for Christmas*** ♪

I'll be home for Christmas
You can count on me
Please have snow and mistletoe
And presents under the tree
Christmas Eve will find me
Where the love light beams
I'll be home for Christmas
If only in my dreams

I was born in Toongabbie

Christmas Eve will find me
Where the love light beams
I'll be home for Christmas
If only in my dreams
If only in my dreams

Recorded in 1943 by Bing Crosby

Our progress was slow. I would make progress with one movement, then it could be days or weeks before I made further progress.
The sister asked me to get a glass out of the cupboard on the wall with my right hand; the hand was all right, the trouble was I hadn't the power in my arm to lift it up. I used to have this bad habit of taking up a challenge. I twisted my body around to the right, turned back quickly flicking the lower part of my arm up onto the door of the cupboard then pressing against it with my fingers to hold my hand there. Then I used my fingers to walk my hand up the door until I reached the handle, then stepped back and pulled the door open. Then I flicked my hand up again onto the shelf and walked my hand over to the glass then let it fall down. Naturally they used to call me 'Wingy'.
I was still in Hospital when The War in the Pacific ended, after the US dropped atomic bombs on Hiroshima. I was down the clinic when the news came over the radio. There were cheers, hugs and tears;

I believe one of the sisters had a brother in the Pacific that would not be coming home.

Bed Pans

Overall, the nurses were a very nice and happy bunch of people and there wasn't a thing the patients (who were able) wouldn't do for them. There was always an exception to the rule though. We had one nurse there who was transferred to our ward who had a very officious attitude' You will do what I say when I say it - you are just the patient here', or that is the way she appeared to me. I asked her for a pan and waited what I considered a reasonable period; then asked again I was told when she was ready'. I waited; still no pan, so I lined three of the other patients up to order a pan at about five minute intervals. When the pans did arrive she came to me first, handed me the pan and said, 'Here' I said, 'I'm sorry nurse - I waited too long the feeling's gone.' She got the same response from the other three.
 I had to hang on till the change of shifts but it was worth it just to see her blood pressure go up; and watch her stamp back through the ward juggling four bedpans.
 After that little incident we all got along famously.

I WAS BORN IN TOONGABBIE

A NIGHT AT THE PICTURES

When I could walk around my right arm hung at my side. When it came to walking up steps I placed my left foot on the step above and lifted my right leg up to meet my left. Going down steps I would place my right foot down then bring my left foot down to meet it. If I had my left foot off the ground and my right knee only slightly bent I would fall over and it was a heck of a job to get up again.
A bloke by the name of Joe Smith from, "Kensington." was two doors up and there was also a bloke named Kelly from "La Perouse." He was in the bed next to me. Joe Smith and I got into a bit of trouble once when another kid came in and left him his clothes. I knew Joe had some clothes in his locker so I said to Joe, 'How about we go to the pictures tonight?' He was keen to go so he agreed. I was just on my feet at that time and still a bit awkward, so, off to the pictures.
 We were sure the nurse would not report us if we came back after the show. They wouldn't put us in; we got on well with them.
My trousers were up around my ankles, and the shirt sleeves were up a bit as they were a bit short on me. Joe had two dropped feet, and he had to lift his legs up high because his toes touched the ground first.
Anyway, off we went. We caught the tram up the hill for about two stops and arrived at The North Sydney Picture Theatre, then purchased our tickets for the

movie and walked into the Picture Theatre. We watched the show and when the movie finished, Joe as usual, was first out high stepping it because of his floppy feet. By the time I got out there, I saw Joe standing between two big chaps in suits. I was up the top of the stairs. I asked, 'What's up Joe?' One of the gentlemen standing with him looked at me, and said to Joe, 'Where's your mate?' Joe said, 'Inside'; I couldn't make a liar out of him, so I just walked straight out the door and took off down the road; it was cold, and I had to walk all the way back to the Hospital, go through the hole in the paling fence and get into bed.

But what we did not know was a new nurse had been transferred to our ward that night, and noted our absence in the report book.

When I got there my bed was stripped.

So I had to go and report to the nurse and ask why my bed was stripped.

'Oh' she said, so they made up the bed and got me into it. Then the next thing Joe comes in.

I said, 'What happened to you?'

He said, 'I come back in the police car, they run me home'

I said, 'You - rotten mongrel!' (I was dirty because I had to walk).

While the nurse was making my bed, she asked how I liked the movie and said, 'I like to see someone with a bit of go in them to stir the place up for awhile'.

The next day I asked Joe what the police said. He told me one of them asked him his name, and when he said 'Joe Smith' they called him a bloody liar.
Anyway Joe got into some trouble with the nurses, and she went him. She believed him to be the leader of the bunch, and blamed him for taking me with him.
Joe tried to convince her that it was my suggestion.
He said, 'Reg was the leader of the bunch, he was the one that suggested it'.
He said, 'Its Reg, he suggested that'.
I said, 'Me suggested what Joe?'
But he had no hope; when he looked over at me for support; I put on a sweet innocent look, and thought that would teach him to leave me stranded at the bottom of the ramp in a wheelchair, the night we nearly ran into the Matron and the Superintendent.
Another nurse came out and she said, 'I'm glad to see something happening round here. It's a dull place and needs some excitement'.
The police went out to inform Mum, and Joe's parents, and when Mum and Mrs. Smith came down to the Hospital they had to face the Superintendent.
 I didn't know much of what was going on, but when Mum came around she said, 'Poor Mrs. Smith, when she got in there he gave her what O, she came out nearly in tears.'
Mum went in (and Mum's motto has always been, the best form of defense is attack) so Mum attacked and she started on them - 'She left her 16 year old boy, and he

was handicapped, he could have fallen under a bus, or anything could have happened to him, and you left him there where he could get clothes.

'I am going to get the Mirror newspapers down on this, and the daily newspapers'.

The Superintendent came right down and assured us that it wouldn't happen again.

Mum left the office and came over to see me, and told me all about having to leave home early and leaving her work. 'Now I have to go home and catch up, have dinner ready for the rest of the family when they arrive home from work'. After telling me this, Mum said to me, 'Don't you do that again to us you bugger.' I said, 'No Mum.'

The Pet

We had an old Scottish nurse there, who was a redhead, and a very big nurse. She used to come round of a morning with the water in the dish for you to have a wash. You had to get into bed, wash yourself all over and change into your clean pajamas under the sheets.

She used to come in the middle of the ward and she would go right down to my bed and she'd pass it, then go down the other end of the ward. Then she would go back and get some more dishes, and go up the other way and give them all their water.

The boys would say, 'Can't you get the water a bit warmer than this?'

She replied, 'It was warm when I left, it takes too long to get here you'll be all right'.
As we were out on the veranda it was cool. She would come out, take all the blankets off the beds to make sure that they all got out and washed quickly, and then they could have their blankets back again.
Then she would get up to my bed and say, 'Are you awake Reg?'
'Yes I'm awake, Scotty'.
She'd say, 'I'll go and get you some warm water now'.
So she would go out and get me some warm water, and that would stir the rest of them up, and I was going to go right along with it.
I wasn't going to have cold water for a wash, if I could get out of it.
So she made me 'the Pet'. I was the envy of them all; she was quite good to me.

18th Birthday Party

Another time it was Kelly's 18th Birthday and he was allowed to go home. He wanted to know if I could come home with him. They would pick me up and yes he got his parent's consent. And yes, they would pick me up and bring me back with them in the car. The Clinic gave him permission to go home and stay overnight, providing he was picked up and returned to the Clinic

I WAS BORN IN TOONGABBIE

by car. Upon his return he was to change into his pajamas, and his clothes were to be taken home. Then he was allowed to go home.

So I went out there to the Party and I had a few beers and I was only 16 at the time. Because everybody out there was drinking, I had a few beers and I was drinking and singing away. When I got into bed, next thing I was asking for a bucket near me.

There was an Aboriginal woman there, and gee she had nice eyes. She was very pleasant, with a happy go' lucky nature.

She came in and she got me the bucket and said, 'Are you sure you're alright mate, are you ok?' Chuckling, I said, 'Yea, I'm Ok. I think'.

Later on, just out of conversation, I told mum (not thinking what I was saying) and what she wasn't going to do to Mrs. Kelly if she got her, giving her son beer.

But she never did anything.

Hospital Visitors

I was playing for North Manly and I was only half way through the season when I went to Hospital. On visiting days about four or five of the girls that used to watch us play footy and go to the dances with us, came to the Hospital to see me.

Problem was, Dad had come to visit me that day, and had to compete with all the girls; it was a bit embarrassing.

So the girls started to talk to Kelly, who was in the bed next to me.

The next weekend, since the girls talked to him, Kelly's up doing his hair and Joe Smith sings out, 'What's up Kelly, is 'Wingy' having visitors this week is he?'

Shallow Waters

We had a bloke in the ward that was an encyclopedia of jokes. I don't think I heard him tell the same joke twice, from one week to the next. We used to call him Shallow-Water as he was very short.

Shallow-Water used to go out from the ward at the weekends to visit his girlfriend, then just before visiting hours, he'd come back to bed in time and she would come back to visit him.

I WAS BORN IN TOONGABBIE

HOME FOR CHRISTMAS

I don't remember getting home for Christmas. I was there for a long time. It started in April so it would have been after Christmas before I came home.
But I was one of the lucky ones that eventually did make it home for Christmas. Although my right arm still hung at my side, and I could not use my right leg to go up steps, I was glad to get away from the hospital and get around despite the handicap. It was not easy being confined to one place when you were as energetic as I was. I don't remember how long I was an outpatient - I know it went on for some time. Social Security if I remember correctly was 5/- (five shillings) a week sickness benefit, which only paid my fares to and from the clinic. My parents still had to feed and clothe me. That's when I had a lot of trouble going around - I had sort of given up, and I couldn't get a job.
What I did learn from this was, if you are willing to try, someone was always there to give you a hand, but if all you did was sit back and complain you were on your own.
I did get down in the dumps though, especially when I tried to iron my shirt with my right hand. At this time I could lift my hand from the elbow. I would take hold of the iron handle but I hadn't the strength to push the damn thing. I would take hold of my right hand with my left, and fling it away wishing it was cut off, so it could not get in the way.

I'm glad I didn't have the courage to have it done; it has come in very handy since those days.

I was in one of those moods when I saw the doctor at the clinic; he listened to what I had to say about it. Complaining about not being able to work, pull my weight like the rest of the family, couldn't join in activities and having to come to the Clinic each day.

That man gave me the best advice that anyone could have given me when he told me to, 'Put on my number 9 boots, turn myself around and give myself a good kick up the rear-end'.

It made me think about what I was going to do about myself; either sit down like a baby and whine about my troubles and bore everyone to death, or put my best foot forward and do something about improving my situation.

I decided on the latter. I started going to Harbord baths through the week so no one would see the wastage in my arm and leg (I was a bit sensitive about it) and gradually I started to swim again, and then started riding a push bike until I could master it.

I WAS BORN IN TOONGABBIE

Dance Challenge

Every one hung out at The Manly War Memorial, where they had dances. I was a bit worried I couldn't swing my arm or do much dancing. I finished up getting the courage to go to the dance, and I went with my friends the Weeklies. I had to get up with one leg and pull the other leg up, and I couldn't get into my fob pocket with my right hand. I had to reach across with my left hand to get my 2/- (two shillings) out to pay for the dance, and the bloke said, 'You don't have to pay if you can't dance' I said, 'I'm going to have a go anyway'
I had to keep the right leg straight and the left leg just hung. I got in there, and started talking, and I borrowed a second handkerchief and made a sling for my arm, which helped me keep my hand on the girls back while I concentrated on keeping my right leg straight, whenever I had to put my weight on it. I mustn't have done too badly as I stayed till the dance hall closed. My friends and I slowly drifted apart, because they still had their football, swimming and dancing.

Dancing again helped me to get confidence in myself. I was always frightened that if any one picked on me I couldn't even look after myself, I met a girl with a problem leg, we used to meet up and talk and we started going out together. I don't know what happened there; she was a nice girl we just drifted apart.

The Crippled Children's Association

Hanging around Manly, I met up with a teenager about my own age. His name was Johnny Bennett. At the time he was getting around on crutches; he had Osteoporosis in the leg. It was a friendship that lasted a number of years; we stuck round as good mates there for a long time.

He introduced me to the Crippled Children's Association which was run by a Miss Jean Garside. We got together once a week, in the basement of a building in Sydney.

They were one of the happiest group of people I have ever known, and that's where I meet Beryl.

We had our outings, and somehow it did not matter that other people looked at you because you were handicapped. We could laugh at our fumbles, and help each other. If help was asked for, you did not have people coming over saying, 'You poor thing; let me help you.' They meant well, but I preferred someone to say do you need a hand mate; and accept your reply.

Everything you could do for yourself was an achievement; no matter how small it was just another step forward.

I WAS BORN IN TOONGABBIE

Johnny Bennet, Reg Rae and Beryl Wyber

KISS AND TELL

We used to go to parties with them. One party we went to had a game to guess the name of your partner. One of the boys suggested you go outside, you gave the girl a big kiss then you came back in again.

So I thought that's all right, and they said to me, now the girls have got to see you, and tell you the number and you tell them which bloke to go with.

Ah' right O, so when they came along they'd turn round and say 'What number have I got?', so I said, 'Well you have to pick a number,' and I would tell them who they were going with.

So they would give me a number and I would tell them who they were going with.

If any good sort would come along and say what number I'd say, '7' (that was my number), is the best. 'Alright', I said, 'number 7.' and out we'd go; any good sorts I told them number 7, and they didn't wake up to it that I was getting all the good ones and they were getting the others.

SAND IN THE FACE

We went down to Royal National Park for a picnic. A whole group of us was there as was one chap there that I didn't know what was wrong with his leg; (he didn't need crouches or a walking stick to get around). He decided that he would have a wrestle with me. We started to wrestle and he finished up on top of me I was going to toss him. I could have tossed him off he was screaming out watch that leg don't hurt that leg.

So I am lying there with him on top of me trying to figure which leg it was and how I was going to get him off without hurting his leg. The next thing Beryl picked up some sand and threw it in his face.

So he got up quickly, trying to get the sand out of his eyes and going crook. And someone said to Beryl, 'you shouldn't have done that.'

She was feeling a bit embarrassed and moved back and back a bit.

I felt, sorry for her (we weren't going together at that stage); I went over, and said, 'It's alright, 'I could have tossed him off.' 'You shouldn't have really done it'. I was just worried about his leg, I didn't know which one but I said, 'Never mind, don't worry she'll be right.'

I WAS BORN IN TOONGABBIE

THE TRAIN RIDE

Going back home, we all got in the train, which was crowded. I had a seat there and everyone else had a seat. Someone said, 'Oh! Where's Beryl?'
'Oh I don't know, she's probably in the other carriages with the rest of them'.
'Well you'd better go and find her; we've got to get her back'.
I said, 'Me?'
They said, 'Yes, go and find her.'
I said, 'Oh – Yea' (I thought that here we go).
They said, 'I think she was heading that way last time I seen her, we'll mind your seat'. So I go through the carriages, and I found her two carriages behind, on her own.
I said, 'What are you doing way back here?'
She said, 'I got lost in the crowd, I couldn't see them.'
I said, 'Come on, we'll go back with the others again'.
I said, 'When the train stops we'll hop out and run back to the carriage and get in. So we ran the 2 carriages and got back on board.
The two people got up from minding the seats, and I got the seat near the window and Beryl got the seat next to me. I thought. 'Hang on, something is going on here, I'm not too sure but I think I'm being trapped'. They must have seen me thinking and they said, 'What's up Skeet, what are you thinking about?'
I said, 'Nothing, not a thing, everything's all right.'

I WAS BORN IN TOONGABBIE

THE ROYAL EASTER SHOW - 1947

Wanda and Beryl talked Johnny Bennett and me into going to the Royal Easter Show.
Well as I said before, mum didn't give me too much money; and I used to go home and ask her what she wanted. That would leave me with just my fares and a few bob to spend. I couldn't save up anything (and it took me years to find out why but eventually I did find out) so I had to go home and had to ask for some extra money for the show.
So at the Royal Easter Show we went on a couple of things with them.
Then they wanted to go in the Ghost House. We said, 'No, we don't want to go in the Ghost House - you go in and we'll wait for you'.
 So we sent them in there, and while they were in The Ghost House, Johnny Bennett and I were outside waiting, and were looking at that part of the Ghost House. We were giving her a wink and trying to coax her into taking her mask off, and she was shaking her head – no. We said, 'Come on give us a look and show your face'.
Anyway we coaxed her into it and she wasn't a bad looking blonde, you could tell she had a good shape in the tight skeleton costume, and then she put the mask back on afterwards.
Beryl and Wanda came out of the Ghost House; she must have seen we were with them and walked away.

I was born in Toongabbie

Dorothy Rae

I WAS BORN IN TOONGABBIE

FINDING WORK AFTER POLIO

I used to know Les Cavanagh there; he went round in the truck to the Fish Markets at Toukley on the Central Coast, and The City Markets. He filleted the fish for the Fish & Chip Shop. I'd go in there and talk to him when he worked for Frank Manson; he didn't mind. In fact I spend so much time in there that he ended up giving me a few jobs.

Lance would get me to put the spuds in the potato peeler (it was like a washing machine with little pimples on the inside, which took all the skin off the potatoes.) You'd pour water through as you went to wash the dirt off them, then slip them into the cutter to shape them into chips; then you'd push the potatoes through into a box lined with butcher's paper till it was full. I would do that now and again, and it finished up with me getting a job there washing up.

I am not sure what happened after that, whether he recommended me or not, but the Fish Shop up the road wanted somebody, so I started working there making the chips, and cooking fish and chips. When the rush was on, I'd get the girl to sit at the till while I watched everybody coming in plus judging how much to cook.

We were flat out taking the orders, cooking the fish and chips, wrapping them up, and then giving them to the girl with the price. She was ringing it up, taking the money and giving the change.

I kept the customers moving along - no one waited for very-long. I worked there for quite a while.

Village Dry cleaners

Later, I got the job at The Village Dry Cleaners, Whistler. St. Manly. My job at the Cleaners was washing anything that couldn't be got out with dry cleaning, and needed careful treatment, plus doing the dry cleaning as well.

They put the clothes into one tank and the dirt would settle down from the clothes to the bottom of the settling tank, which was a 44-gallon drum. He wanted me to take the tank with the sludge in it, put it in the Van and take it to the tip at Balgowlah. You could only carry a third of the tank at a time as it was very heavy.

I didn't tell them I had Polio, but wondered how the hell I was going to get it down there as I couldn't bend my leg. So I maneuvered it so I could put the stiff leg down first, have it straight then bring the other one down to meet it; then I could hold on to something with my hand to help.

When I got to the tip I just backed the Van up to where it had to be dumped, pull it down and let it go. He got very stroppy there after a while, so I threw it in and went to work for Little's Dry Cleaners.

They asked me what I earned at The Village Dry Cleaners. So I told them what it was clear and they gave

me a bit extra. They put me into spotting at Manly for a while, and then they sent me to their big Factory at Balgowlah which was an old Service Station at the time. I got along well with them and they were good people to work for.
I think it was about this time that Beryl and I broke up for a while.
I said, 'I don't know and I was getting tired'.
I was still at Little's Dry Cleaners, and I think the split between us lasted about a fortnight.
As a result she was snappy at home and I was starting to get a bit snappy too.
I tried hanging out with the boys who I used to have fun with before; but they had girls now and it wasn't fun anymore.
I was getting miserable, and starting to miss her company, so I rang her up first and then we were both happy after that.

Courting

When I was going out with Beryl, She would say to mum, 'Why don't you give him more pocket money?' He's got nothing, he's always broke'.

I WAS BORN IN TOONGABBIE

Mum said, 'Well I know now that you are after my son, and not just his money, because he hasn't got any, so if you really like him you'll stick around'.

I had my license and Bert decided to lend me his 1926 Essex.
Bert said, 'Take Beryl for a run in the Essex'.
So were driving along through the back streets down to Curl Curl in the old 1926 Essex; I found they were very hard to steer and changing the gears was awkward. Beryl was telling me about something funny she read in the newspaper. I couldn't make out just what she said so I turned around and said, 'What did you say?'
While I was turning to hear what she said at the same time I turned the wheel and when I looked up there's a post straight in front of me. Swerving to miss it, we went straight up the gutter over the side and down the bank, and finished with the car upside down.
We were alright, but the windscreen was smashed, and the canvas hood was damaged.
Some people who lived across the road let us use the phone, to get a message to tell Bert.
I told him that I had a bit of an accident with the car and it's not going too well, and I told him where I was.
So Bert arrived with a couple of spanners, and found his cherished car turned upside down – smashed. After a few choice words, we rolled it over onto its feet.
At the time a farmer visiting his friends there said, 'I've got a windscreen for a 1926 Essex down the garage; I'll

send it up and you can just pay me for the postage.' I thanked him very much for that.

In the meantime Bert found another windscreen so I had to pay for that one too (which left with me with even less pocket money).

So when the other one arrived he gave it away to Ambros McIvaine, he didn't care he had another one - he didn't have to pay for it.

Then I had to get the canvas and make a new hood for the Essex. However, firstly we had to pull the damaged hood off, and laid it out so we had a pattern to work from.

We had it on the big industrial sewing machine with the large sewing needle, and we made a damn good job of it. So it ended up he had a better looking hood than he had before.

We were working on it every week-end, and Beryl keep coming over to see me every week end. It was getting a bit monotonous, and she was asking how long this was going to take, but she still kept coming around. I couldn't do anything about it, because it was my fault.

Beryl's mother: Annie (Topsy) had re-married John Burkhardt in 1942, after Beryl's dad had died 1936 from TB.

In July 1948 they sold the house at 11 Clark Street, packed up and moved 65 miles down the south coast into the Hinterlands. They were going into shares with John's brother Bill and his wife Dot, to run a

Guesthouse called "Laurel Park" at Burradoo, and Beryl had to go with them.

So we wrote letters to one another, which wasn't so hot. Anyway she finished up coming back and living with her Aunt Martha in Leichhardt, Sydney they lived above a shop. Martha's husband John Jack looked after the tennis courts at the back of the shop. Beryl found a job working at Bennett & Wood Pty Ltd, manufacturer of Speedwell Cycles and spare parts.

I used to go down to Bennett & Woods so I could see her; she worked there as an operator on the big computers, calculating and making up the bills. The computers were giant things then; now they're only small and they can do the same job.

So I went there and got a job as a Store-man, and I was working there for a while.

Marriage 1950

I remember: before we were married, we made an appointment with a Macquarie Street Specialist, to find out if Beryl could have children.

When the result was in, and we found out she could we were so happy that when we left the Specialist we could have hugged one another, but in those days it was not something you did in public.

I WAS BORN IN TOONGABBIE

We were crossing the road when suddenly a car jammed on its brakes, and came screeching to a stop right in front of us, and we found ourselves in the middle of the road. If I remember it was an old 1926 Chevy with the canvas hood.
The bloke leaned out the window with a grin on his face and said, 'You don't want to let her get you that bad mate!' I just gave him a grin and waved.
We were just so pleased with the results we just didn't know what we were doing, so we had to be more careful. Beryl didn't believe in sex before marriage, and I respected her for that. We didn't want to get pregnant before marriage.
 This gave us a chance to get to know each other and form a better bond, and I think we were better for it.

In 1949-1950 Churches & halls were hard to get.
Churches were very busy with weddings; people got married in churches and had the reception in the hall afterwards. The halls also held dances on Saturday nights; it was a regular thing, as well as holding various other functions.
People around said you couldn't get halls or Churches as you wanted them, they had to be booked well in advance.
Beryl wrote to her mother at 'Burradoo' the Guest House at Laurel Park. Her mum wrote back and told Beryl that she would make all the arrangements and it was alright.

I was born in Toongabbie

We got a week off from work and were married, on 19th August 1950, at The Wesley Chapel, in Sydney.
 The Reception was held at Cahill's in Pitt Street.
Beryl wanted me to sing 'The Anniversary Song' when we were doing the 'Bridal Waltz'.
Me! I couldn't sing in front of people, or get up on stage.
(The bride and groom do the first lap alone then the others join in after that was finished).
But that night when I held her in my arms, all I could see was her face and I could sing.
 I was so happy, and I sang the whole lot through for her while we danced around the floor with the entire crowd was around us, and it didn't worry me one bit.

I was born in Toongabbie

♫ 'The Anniversary Song' ♫

Oh, how we danced on the night we were wed
We vowed our true love, though a word wasn't said
The world was in bloom, there were stars in the skies
Except for the few that were there in your eyes

Dear, as I held you close in my arms
Angels were singing a hymn to your charms
Two hearts gently beating, murmuring low
"Darling, I love you so"

The night seemed to fade into blossoming dawn
The sun shone anew but the dance lingered on
Could we but recall that sweet moment sublime
We'd find that our love is unaltered by time

Dear, as I held you close in my arms
Angels were singing a hymn to your charms
Two hearts gently beating, murmuring low
"Darling, I love you so"

Al Jolson and Saul Chaplin with music by Iosif Ivanovici

I WAS BORN IN TOONGABBIE

Beryl & Reg Rae

Honeymoon

We went to Toronto on Lake Macquarie just south of Newcastle, for our honeymoon, and we stayed in a boarding house not far from the Station.
Our room and window opened onto the front veranda. A miner, his wife and kids they lived there permanently.
His kids were out there playing on the front veranda and Beryl was laying on the bed and said, 'Come and give me a cuddle,'
I said, 'Oh, I don't know; the kids on the veranda are making me nervous'.
Beryl said, 'They won't see us having a cuddle.'

I said, 'Oh, I don't know.' and I walked over near the bed.
Next thing the blinds were rattling then, Zip! Zip! Up they go, and I looked over at the window and a little head comes through.
Next thing someone yelled out, 'Hey what are you doing, get out of there' and the kid gets his head out of the window.
I said, 'That was close, wasn't it?'
After the honeymoon we moved into a boarding house and rented a room in Manly. We both travelled back and forth to work for about 4 months.
Then they gave us a single room with two single beds, but that was no good to Beryl; she pushed the beds together. I was a bit embarrassed about them coming in and seeing the bed changed, but she wasn't.

First Home

On leaving the boarding house we went down to Falls Creek near Nowra. We had bought a 4-acre property on the Princes Highway; it was just past the Huskisson turn off.
 So that's what was happening to my pocket money and why I didn't have any; Mum had saved it for this.

Then we bought another 4 acres from the brother in-law Bert Guest. He and my sister Joyce had already built a shack, which was built out of car box wood down there. Having sold the 4 acres property and shack to us they then bought more acres further up the road.

So we now owned a shack on an 8-acre property.

We'd saved about £200 to get started on building the house; and we had moved our bed and some furniture into the shack for accommodation until the house was built.

Bert had already dug down 6ft and had a well there; but it never had any water in it at any time. It was dug through clay and never likely to. He went crook when I used to fill it up with rubbish. I said, 'It's my place not yours.'

Bert would come down to visit in his dirty work clothes, and not thinking sit on the end of our bed dirtying the blankets.

With no water tank, water was in short supply, so we collected water with whatever we could. Washing became a problem, especially a large blanket.

I put a partition up so when you opened the door it blocked the bed off and Bert got grouchy on that, because he didn't have anywhere to sit and couldn't sit on our bed.

We started to clear the land, and for entertainment at night we had a board with a blanket over it that we sat on, with a small bonfire in front of us to keep warm.

I WAS BORN IN TOONGABBIE

We'd sit in front of the fire and listen to our songs played on a wind up gramophone. The gramophone was given to us by Beryl's brother-in-law Bill Pedersen, and it was given to him for some drawings that he did for an Officer on the boats.

Bath time was in a 44-gallon drum with the top cut off, and propped up on bricks, so we could light a small fire to warm the water in the drum. Later on we bought a real galvanized tin bath. For privacy to block it off from the street I had a two-man tent, that I used to have in my single days, and threw it over the bath. We had enough room to have a bath and get dressed then duck inside.

We put the light outside so we could see and would have our hot bath in there that was our bathroom.

Our cooking area was outside; to protect us from the weather the cookhouse was closed in with off cuts of corrugated iron and a door so we could keep the animals out at night. We were quite happy; it wasn't perfect but it was all right.

Down the backyard we had half a dozen white leghorn chooks, which we had penned in. Later we decided to get a rooster for the hens so we could have chickens.

The hens didn't like the young rooster and pecked a hole in his wing, and it started to bleed so I had to take him out, and I didn't know what the heck I was going to do with him.

I WAS BORN IN TOONGABBIE

So I fed him up near the house, and at night we put him in the lean to. That was our cooking area and kitchen, out the back..

At first, we didn't have a stove; so I got a second hand fuel stove and packed around it with clay, and that's where we did our cooking outside bringing it inside to eat.

At night, it was a race between the rooster and me, to see who got in the door first. If he won I use to take him outside and try and beat him to the door again.

Eventually the rooster's wing healed, so I put him back in with the hens. By this time he was a bit older and he was the boss of the yard. Then the hens left him alone.

Mr. Green was our neighbor - he lived across the road and was a builder. We gave him the £200 to build the house and I helped him.

In due course the house was built; I also had the piers set out at the front of the house ready to put a lounge room on later. Our two bedroom home had a small kitchenette with an open red brick fire-place and a small bathroom. The laundry was out the back, along with our toilet, which was a hole dug in the back yard. There was no electricity or water connected to the house. Things were starting to look up when I built a tank stand, from abandoned Army blockades that were tapered concrete blocks used on the beach to stop enemy vehicles. I put a wooden base on top and a water tank on top of that, did all my own plumbing, and fenced off the four acres around the house.

2002 Photo of "Elimatta" home at Falls Creek

The Partnership

There wasn't much work around at the time, but there was cordwood cutting, for the kiln ovens at the brick works.
Bert and I went into partnership cutting the cordwood, but he wasn't as keen and quite often not around to help. It was all right for him as he had a pension to fall back on. Well that soon split up.

I WAS BORN IN TOONGABBIE

Work Camp

I had nothing until I got a job as a waiter, at HMAS Albatross airbase, Albatross, Gladiator Road, Nowra in the works and housing camp. Here they housed and fed up to 200 workers on the base. You had to be there for breakfast, dinner and tea. It was too far to go home in between shifts so I had to stay there for each shift, and didn't get home till 8 o'clock at night, but the money was good.

That was going fine until the boss and his wife went away on a holiday and made me headwaiter. I was 22 at the time, when I was confronted by old Jim; old Jim was a crabby old bachelor who let his dog run freely around the place. He came into the room and took temporary charge. He started laying down the law to everyone stating that will stay there, and we will wash the tea towels afterwards, you will do this, and you have extra things to do and no one was going home until everything is done etc.

Bert comes in with all the answers to defeat old Jim. He was talking to the other two waiters saying, 'You work straight to your time, you don't start before time you start on time, and you finish on time. If you can't get it all done then Jim will just have to do it himself.' Then Bert suggested going on strike if he doesn't like it.

I thought, 'This isn't right' so I said, 'Look you can't do this, and you can't organize a strike'.

I WAS BORN IN TOONGABBIE

Bert said, 'Yes, yes you're quite within your rights to do so', and he talked them into it.

I said, 'Are you fellows going along with this?' and they both said, 'Yes'.

I said, 'Alright then, I will go along with you, but I don't like it.'

Well, that was all Jim wanted, because he came into the kitchen and stood there while I served the staff and took the food orders for the workers.

I said, 'Look I am sorry, but I have to go along with them, they're going to work for only 2 hours'. Usually we come in a bit earlier so we can take the orders having it cooked and ready to serve the men.

Any way Jim put on an act and he blamed me for everything I got the blame for the lot.

I said, 'Now wait a minute - the two cooks said go out!'

I said, 'I can't stand and take that', so I went out and laid it out to them, in front of all the men too and he walked straight out the door, he had me.

Next thing, I was sacked, Bert came in. Don't collect your pay when the boss comes back - it will be fixed up. It was never fixed up, they did ask him if I would have been sacked he said no, I believed I was gone, and they had a replacement for me. Anyway they drove my pay out to me.

That's when I got a job at the Buttons Dry cleaners at Nowra and I worked there for quite awhile.

I WAS BORN IN TOONGABBIE

OUR FIRST CHILD

June 9, 1951; our first child Lorraine came along. Beryl was admitted to Royal North Shore Hospital for a Caesarian Section on June 7, 1951. I had to turn around and wait at home. The time was near and I was waiting for a phone call. And that's when they said, 'Is there something wrong with you.
You're expecting a kid; you're supposed to be waiting for the phone to ring and walking up and down hallway smoking cigarettes'.
 I was thinking, 'I wonder what's happening?' I wonder how she's going and I completely forgot about cigarettes. I was too busy thinking about what Beryl was going through. Anyway I got the phone call; it was about 1 or 2 O'clock when I got the message. I couldn't go straight away because it would have left others in a spot for work; they let me off work about a week or so later. I finally went up to the Hospital to see her, but she was already out and recovering at her sister Dot's place. Beryl came home on 24th June.

I WAS BORN IN TOONGABBIE

Lorraine Beryl Rae

BUTTON'S

I was working at 'Button's' Dry cleaners in Nowra.
I had to ride about 20 km (about 12 miles) each day, back and forward on my pushbike – rain, hail or shine, from Falls Creek to Nowra.
I was working in there doing spotting and cleaning for them. I worked there for quite a long time. It was around that time when the bush fires came through.

THE FIRE-STORM

It was a hot day in Feb 1952 when a phone call came through, and the Boss told me to get home; the bush fires were raging down there. I had to get on my pushbike and ride home. As I was getting to the turn off to the Albatross Naval Base Aerodrome the smoke was that thick you couldn't see your way on the road. I had to get home. I knew the road was straight so I took a deep breath and I pedalled like blazes. I couldn't hold my breath all the way, and when I got out the other side I was coughing and spluttering.

It took about 30 seconds before I stopped coughing and was all right again, but I still kept going. I filled my lungs with fresh air and after a while was ok.

When I got home the place was still standing. The fire was that bad it was throwing big hunks of bark well ahead of it and the heat was so terrific, they'd call it a firestorm today.

Although you couldn't see the flames you could feel your face drying out and starting to burn.

By this time our house was in trouble and I couldn't do anything about it.

The firefighters said, 'Do you want us to back burn?'

But it was too late; I couldn't do anything for the house. I said: 'there are people that live behind us, and if I back burned to try and save our place and they're making a dash to get out, they will be trapped and I couldn't take the risk'.

So I went around letting the chooks out. I couldn't get to the gate on the chicken run, so to give them a chance I pulled the bird wire off the side of the chicken coop.

I WAS BORN IN TOONGABBIE

But then I had to run because I was burning - we all had to clear out.

Next thing our house went, the whole lot of it.

After the fire had passed there was a mat on the grass untouched; the grass was still green under it.

The chooks did not escape. They were dead, all in a line as they were running away. The heat I think was just too intense; the fire got to their lungs and burnt them out.

We had 3 days and 2 nights of fighting fires.

All we could do was just a burn a firebreak between us and the fire and get it going into the fires. We had the old bush rakes to rake up the leaves, to light a fire and a big flap to belt out the fires once we had burned a path between the fires, then we had to run and leave, because of the heat that radiated from them.

Each night we did that, and it stopped a lot of the fires and saved a lot of houses that way.

When we were tired we just hopped into a drum of cold water, and it woke us up to keep going.

There was one chap who came to fight the fire wearing shorts, and rubber gumboots. I don't know how he could have worn them, with no protection from the heat. He got a spark down his gumboot; next thing he threw his rake down, and he's yelling and jumping around trying to put the spark out. He stamped his foot straight down on an up-turned rake, and it went straight through his gumboot up into his foot.

He got it out and he was doing a bit of cursing and all we could do was laugh at seeing his antics, and for being so stupid. Another time you would have been more serious and sympathetic about it, but we were so tired; we asked him to show us again how he done it.

Prior to that the RSL Club, came around with a keg of warm beer to drink.
They asked me and I said, 'No thanks, I'll go to sleep'.
The Salvation Army came round and they had a stick through the handle of a 4 gallon kerosene can full of tea. I went for the tea because it gave you more of a pick up the beer only made you sleepy.
We were so tired; we got to the end of it and we found that there was an old sandstone track built through the scrub for the trucks to go through, leading to some place there.
I was sitting on a rock relaxing because the fires were all burnt out but we had to be there in case of flare ups.
A little bloke from the Nowra Pub, a waiter, had his black trousers on with the black band and white shirt and a black bow tie (which he took off later). Bert was sitting beside us we were having a break. The waiter came up and said, 'Would you like a drink?'
Bert said, 'Yea' and he threw it down, 'Ah, that's good'.
He said, 'Here Reg, have a drink'.
'Oh yea' I didn't think about it, it was Brandy. I was dry enough; I didn't want that stuff down my neck.

I said, 'Thanks, but that's plenty - I don't want any more of that'.

So we moved along further and got to a place where there was another group.

Another fire fighter and I went and lay down on the side of the road and the rocks felt like an innerspring mattress. We were so tired we were both lying there with our heads down, and I was damn near asleep when the bloke next to me gives me a nudge.

He said, 'That bloke over the other side of the road with his brush', (one of the fresh chaps to stop the fire from crossing) he noticed his trousers are on fire. You could see it was smoldering at the back.

I said, 'Tell him'

He said, 'No, you tell him'.

I looked up (I was that damned tired I didn't have a yell in me).

I said, 'Bugger it, he'll find out soon enough' and we stuck our heads down.

When it got up passed his boots, he started to feel the heat, and he turned round and worked it out.

Next thing he was yelling and doing a bit of a dance, and we had a bit of a chuckle about that, but he was all right.

I WAS BORN IN TOONGABBIE

AFTER THE FIRE

It was amazing. People came down from everywhere offering to help us and offering us a place to stay after the fire. All we had left was what we were standing in. Beryl only had the old working clothes she stood in and I just had my working clothes. Everything else was gone and all Lorraine had was a nappy and a singlet and that's all. Some organization came down with clothes to see if they would fit us. Everything else was gone too; all our furniture, the gun barrel lying across the table was melted over the table. The crystal decanter set that Jack gave us as a Wedding gift, had melted down the brick works of the fireplace; we couldn't save a damn thing.
One farmer came down and told us that there was room up at his place.
His mother said to let us know that she had a sewing machine and she would help us make and sew dresses and things.
 I thanked him very much, but we had got an offer to rent a large garage cheaply up the street that had a kitchen with a stove and a bedroom in it, and the telephone and fireplace and the laundry outside. We decided we would be better off on our own and we took that. (It was just up from my sister Joyce & my in-law, Bert's place).
One night I came home and found that someone had been around, because they had left us some clothes and also there was some for Lorraine. Another night by the

time I got home it was dark, and because there were no streetlights, I went to the door and 'Bang', I hit something. I'd walked straight into this really nice dining room table set. They just left it there because nobody was at home.

People came from everywhere to help us - it was amazing. They even took up collections of money to help us rebuild our place. Then the crowds of timber getters came down from Tomarone a large family of them. They were in the timber business; they had bullocks, drays and timber jiggers. The Apex Club came down too, and they set to work to cut the timber on our land then drag the logs out with the bullock onto the road to put them on the jiggers. Then it was taken to the Mills, who cut them up for nothing and gave us what we needed. They also hauled it back again all for nothing and organised teams to go and put it together again. The Mill did all right out of that as well; they kept what we didn't need.

Albatross Naval Base

After the bush fires I finished up leaving there because Green and I got a job at the Albatross Naval Air Base, Nowra and I would catch the bus up with him.

I started working at The "Albatross" Naval Base building aircraft engine test stands. I would catch a bus to work with Mr. Green. It got so cold up there that you had to

have a fire burning to keep you warm to do any work at all. You had to warm up your hands first before you could pick a nail up to put it in, and then knock it in. Then you had to warm your hands up again, to pick up the next nail. By the time you picked up your hammer to knock it in, the nail would fall out of your hands it was just so cold. Before you could sign for anything you had to hold the pen with two hands to stop shaking.
I soon traded that job in to work at the Hawkins Dry cleaners and laundry on the Albatross Naval Base.

Timber!

We had a family of timber getters from Tomarong, a family of them, and blokes from Apex Club came down to help cut the timber. I was helping to cut the trees for timber for rebuilding our home, and some of these blokes some of them were funny. They got around one big stringy bark tree and they were going around it like a beaver. It came to the point where every time the wind blew it creaked and they all scattered. When nothing happened they came back. It was about 12 inches round and perfectly balanced, and still standing.
Bert came down. He had been working with another group.
He said, 'Put a stake in Skeet, where she's going to fall',

I said, 'Bloody way that's going, and the way you're going about it, the roads too hard I can't put one in'.
Bert said, 'No, it's going to go this way'.
I said, 'It's going to go that way towards the road'.
So we laid our bets down.

Suddenly a breeze came and away she went, it didn't go on the road because another tree stopped it falling on the road, it got hooked right up the top in the first fork of the tree.

Then an athletic bloke crossed the road. He was an amateur boxer; he went up to the top of the tree and was cutting it loose.

A bloke said, to me 'How's he going to get down?'

I said, 'He will come down with the tree and just before it hits the ground he'll jump off. It's like jumping off a little step. I have done it myself, you have to be agile you can do it, but you have to keep your axe to your side when you jump and make sure you jump up hill and not down in case the log rolls on you. If you think YOU'RE going to have a bit of trouble you throw your axe away from you'.

Re-Building

The Brickworks also donated the bricks we ordered. When they delivered the timber from the mill it was wet, and they couldn't get onto the block so they off-loaded it

on the side of the highway. I couldn't leave it there because it was too easy for someone to take, or someone could have had an accident by running into it in the dark, and then I would have been in all sorts of trouble. So I put on my raincoat, and I went down there to shift it myself onto the block. Next thing Beryl came down.
I said, 'Ah, what are you doing down here?'
She said, 'I just wanted to help' and she looked up at me a little hurt.
I couldn't knock her back, so I said, 'Alright, love: you get one end of the timber and I'll get the other, and we'll carry it up one piece at a time'.
It was wet and dark and it was hard work and I was worried about her back, because of a curve in her spine. It was slower than I wanted, but we were together, and that meant more than anything to both of us. Helping each other out, we did get all the timber up eventually even though I had to stop for a few rests because I was worried about her.
The plumber in Nowra was selling us iron for the roof, and a friend of Beryl's came down to see us. He was a plumber himself and said 'That's unbranded iron'.
I said, 'It looks alright - look's good',
He said, 'Yes, but it's unbranded and it's good stuff but is not 100%'.
So I rang them up, and went in and told them about it, so they had done their sheets and lost our job.
The friend supplied us with the iron for the roof, and we gave him our building number because he took it off

another job, so he could re-order and get the stuff back for his job. Ended up I had all this nice iron to make a shed, and everyone was a bit envious. We hoped to have the place finished by 8-hour weekend (Oct 1952)

A DOG NAMED MIKE

Beryl got a dog - I don't know where it came from. It was a nondescript looking thing, and it was a fairly large dog. I suppose it stood a metre high or a bit more, had floppy ears, was brown and black and had big paws. It was the most useless dog I've ever come across. If a burglar came round the place it would probable lick them to death, and show them were all the good stuff was, not that we had any good stuff at that stage. We had a few chooks and chickens and it uses to go out with the chickens that were running in the back yard. The dog loved those chickens and uses to put its paw on them and lick them and wash them clean by this time, until they were gasping for breath. We had to take them and put them in the fuel stove that wasn't alight and still a little bit warm to dry them off to revive them. Then off they'd go again chirping and running around.

I was born in Toongabbie

Monday Dec 15, 1952

That was the only time that Beryl lied to me.
To this day I don't know why, but I said, 'Don't come down with my lunch today,' and she said, 'No, I won't'.
I made her promise to stay there and I would come home for lunch. We would both go down together after lunch.
She asked, 'Why?'
I said, 'I just had this feeling of panic for some reason'.
I just didn't want her to go, and I didn't know why. I was frightened and couldn't tell her why.
She said yes but it was the only lie she ever told me.
The day started off routinely. I was down there on my own working on the house, and then a mate called in, asking for help with a job. Afterwards we had a few Christmas drinks..

Yeah…

It was the first time that she said one thing and meant another; she turned round and decided to come down with my lunch.
 Beryl had been walking down the highway pushing Lorraine in a stroller; they were about thirteen minutes into the fifteen minute journey.
What happened next, only Beryl knew?
The truck, on its way to Nowra was loaded with empty petrol drums. The driver put his foot on the brakes and

I WAS BORN IN TOONGABBIE

came to a stop. The young male driver wearing thick eye glasses was in shock.

My Sister Joyce was there in the ambulance with Beryl when she sent Beau her son, to tell me; Beryl had been hit by a truck, but he couldn't find me. A friend found me later on and took me into Nowra Hospital.
I went in. The Police were there, and our neighbors daughter, Trainee nurse, 16 year old Julie Rigby. She was with me when I identified Beryl.
(Julie's mother had re-married Mr. Green the builder across the road)
I saw Beryl and I sort of knew; I saw the tubes on her, and she was just lying there not moving.
 I couldn't see her breathing or anything, but I still had to ask.
 They told me that she had definitely died.
I went back to Joyce's where Beau asked me how she was, and I had to tell him she had died, but I was a broken man after that.

1:30 p.m. Wednesday Dec 17, 1952

The Funeral Service was held at A. S. Cole's Funeral Parlor, Wollongong then proceeded to the Woronora Crematorium.

My mother and Beryl's mother made all the arrangements for the funeral and things. I was glad I had those people there to make the arrangements for me.

I was pretty hopeless at the time; I didn't know what was going on.

We went to the funeral at Wollongong. I was standing up all right waiting to go in, and then afterwards I was sitting out there on the veranda, and there wasn't a tear or anything, but I wasn't talking either.

Lorraine was only 18 months old at the time, and she came up to me and put her arm around me, and I grabbed her, and that's when I broke down, and I couldn't stop again.

Beryl was only 25 when she died, and it really hurt.

You don't meet them like her now. We never had a fight and we could always sit down and talk it over, no matter what was said, or done. There was no anger, no hate.

Life without Beryl

An inquest was held on Jan 9, 1953. The finding was accidental death and no blame was attached to the driver, 20 year old Sidney Mathie, and his passenger, a women from Milton a Mrs. Dorothy Petty.

Everyone was really angry with this result, and found it hard to accept since some of the findings didn't quite add up.

I was still working at HMAS Albatross Dry Cleaners when I had a day off to go to Wollongong to see the solicitors.

One of the naval blokes said, 'I will take you up as the wife and I are going to Sydney and I'll drop you off there'. So I said, 'Righto'.

He picked me up, and I went up to Wollongong and saw the solicitor, and got the train back.

Not long afterwards I finished my job at the Albatross drycleaners, got Lorraine, and went back up to mums for a while at Harbord. I had been up there for about a week or so, when Bert drove up.

He said, 'You'd better get back down there to Nowra; they're talking about getting a team together and finishing that place of yours, then once it's all done you can sell it or do what you like with it afterwards, you had better get down there and help them'.

I went down there and I couldn't find anything that was arranged, so I got a carpenter, a mate of mine; he worked cheap at the weekends. I worked with him to finish the place off, and I paid him each day when it was finished. Mum and Dad sold up and they came down to live in the house at Falls Creek, and to look after Lorraine.

Tasmania 1953

I found it a bit hard to get a job around Nowra, so I went out with Green for a while doing a bit of plumbing and odd jobs around the place. I wasn't coping too well, and Mum said to me 'You'd better go for a trip over to Tassie and see your brother Bill. 'Stay with him and have a good time over there'.
They bought my house and the 4 Acres, and I flew over to Tasmania to see Bill and stayed there.
I was going around the place, and I liked it.
I still carried a photo of Beryl in my wallet. All I knew was I couldn't get close to anyone. I felt like I was a bit of a traitor.
 It took me awhile to get a job, and then I decided I would bring Lorraine over and she could stay with Bill and Aileen. They could look after her and I could work with her there.
 Mum and Pop brought Lorraine over, but I couldn't understand why she wouldn't talk to anyone, and why she always wanted to be near me. She was always fighting Bill and Aileen's two kids; it just wasn't working out.

I WAS BORN IN TOONGABBIE

I could see Lorraine wasn't happy, so I rang mum and pop and asked them to come over and pick her up - she wasn't happy here.

So I went on; and I did meet a girl over there. Her name was Dawn - she was engaged to a fisherman but we were getting very close. She was a nice kid, but she was starting to fight with her fiancée.

I thought 'You're a nice kid but you're a bit young, and it's not fair for me to go there and ask her to look after a 3 or 4 year old kiddy'.

I was all twisted at the time. I left my job at the 7 Ways Dry Cleaners in Wynyard, and. I went looking for a job. I found one at the Nor-West Dry cleaners in Burnie and I boarded in the Somerset Hotel at the time.

Always in the back of my mind though, I had to get back and see Lorraine, or build a place in Tasmania, but Mum and Pop weren't happy to live in Tassie,

It was too cold for them. They were old and they didn't like the climate, and I could understand that part.

All I could hope for was that Lorraine could be settled. I could come back and see her and she could contact me if she needed me. I was there where she could get in touch with me.

I had my chance to get married over there more than once, but I had to keep ducking because I didn't know what I was doing, and I didn't know how the hell things were going to work out.

I kept writing and sending money to Mum to care for Lorraine. Next thing I know Lorraine's with Bert and Joyce; I found that out afterwards.
So I thought 'O well, maybe Joyce will look after her and she might be happy there'. It seemed to go all right for a while but next thing I got a letter from Bert. He wanted half my wages, full adoption, and I was not to come near Lorraine. I was not to come near her at all, and I was to get right out of her life. I said, 'I couldn't take that; I needed to come and see that she was all right'.
So I wrote back and I said, 'No, I would like to be able to see her, and make sure that she is all right'.
I got a letter back saying, that he was sick of arguing with me and your mother through the post, and would I come and get her.
So I sent the money to Mum and Pop and asked them to go and pick Lorraine up. Because of the letter, apparently there were more arguments still going on at home. Joyce still wanted Lorraine she was genuine enough, but Bert was the boss and she had to follow him.
So I stayed in Tasmania. I was going to build a place there and give her a home to come when she wanted to, and be where she could be happy and know where I was.
 It made it awkward for me to ever get really tied up with anyone. Any decent girls I didn't want to tie up.
Well, thinking back; Mum wanted money for school, so I sent her money for uniforms for school. Then I'd come

home every year to see Lorraine in my holidays. The first time I saw Lorraine I was asleep in the lounge room. I remember Lorraine coming home from school and standing there looking at me I turned and said, 'Hello'. I went to put my hand out to her but she stepped back and I thought, 'I can't touch you yet; you have got to touch me first'.

Lorraine went in to see Nan and said to her, 'Is that my real father?' and she said, 'Yes'.

Somerset Hotel Burnie Tasmania: Reg Rae and mates

Woy Woy

I use to write to Lorraine regularly, then the welfare department people came down to see Mum, I don't know who sent them down or why. They wanted to know if I came to see her and if. I sent money home, which I did sometimes by cheque and sometimes by cash.
Lorraine came out and showed them the letters I wrote and said, 'This is the letters my dad wrote.' I was glad that she did that: and they left.
After that I thought, 'No, it's not going to work out I had better get home'. I was well established in Tassie, and I had a lot of good friends down there.
So I came back to Woy Woy. There were a lot bludgers and no - hopers around the place, and I just seem to keep running into them.
They were a different lot of people altogether here than the people in Tasmania, and that hung heavy on my heart for a long time.
While trying to get work Prime Minister Menzies had a credit squeeze on at the time. If you weren't local, and you and weren't in the know, you couldn't get a job down there.
There were jobs about, but you had to be fit. It was no good for me with my Polio - I wouldn't have lasted.
I went up to Hornsby Hospital and got a job working in the laundry. However the job of heaving the heavy wet sheets and clothes about, and pulling and putting them in and out of baskets all the time got too much for me in

the finish. So I left there. My next job was going around collecting for the pensioner funeral fund. I got 10% of whatever I collected. I'd go to the Pensioner Hall in Woy Woy and collect, then to Long Jetty where I started to make house calls, all the way to the Entrance and back. But I never got much out of it, and they cut out my unemployment benefits.

So I went into the Welfare office in Gosford, and complained that I was earning less than what I did on the unemployment benefits a fortnight. They said, 'That's too bad; we're not here for you to start a business'.

So I spoke to them; I said: 'I should get something; I am being honest about it and telling you what I get I need you to make up the difference.

They said, 'Well you will have to go up to Newcastle'.

So I saved my money and I went up to Newcastle, saw them up there, and I was arguing with them. They said, 'They will send someone out to see you; I'm not up to this'.

They sent me out a young boy, who just sat there dumb - eyed while I was talking, and I could see it was a waste of time telling him about what had happened.

Around 1960 I worked at Gosford's Kings Clothing Factory, pressing the clothes they made, and that's where I meet a very good and longtime friend named Joe Cooper.

New Beginnings

13 Springwood Ave Blackwall Mountain, Woy Woy from left Laurice Hawkins, Reg Rae & Lorraine Rae

I wrote to the minister in charge of Welfare, Social Security. They came down to visit me, talked to me, had a look at the house and they sent me to Mount Wilga training School just out of Hornsby. It was at that time, I met and married Laurice Hawkins on 27th October 1962 we had 3 children (Greg, Amanda and Debbie.) That's when I started to do Accountancy. While I was there I got 3 months on-the-job training at Sterling Brothers Hardware Shop at West Gosford working in the office. I did get a good reference from them; they ran me through everything.

After 3 months that was it; I had finished my training and I had to get a job, so I wrote letters but I had to bring in some money so I had to go on Welfare again till I got a job.

My wife Laurice was working at Wally Bruce's butchers in Gosford, and I was getting 2 shilling and 5 pence a fortnight; that was embarrassing for me.

So I sat down and I wrote to everybody. I finished up getting a reply from The Main Roads at Brooklyn. I went there to work but the problem was I had to have a driving license to get to work. I'd let my license slide when I was in Tasmania, and I didn't transfer it over here.

I said, 'Could you hold it for a week?' I went over to Laurice's Dad, Keith Hawkins. He took me for driving experience for a week in his Holden. After this I did my test again, got my license, and started at Brooklyn as a Clerical Laborer.

Laurice had £400 (or $800), and bought the block of land up North Gosford in Henry Parry Drive. So from then on I asked her how much she needed to keep the house running. Anything after that went into buying and building the house. We both dug the foundations; I hired a cement mixer, and ordered a ready cut house to lock up stage to make it quicker and easier to assemble. But they didn't supply all the material at one go; I wrote a letter asking them why. They said, 'That they didn't

send out all the material all at once, that they only delivered as you needed it, but they went bust and I had a lot of trouble there and I didn't get all the money back.
I hired a bloke to help to put the frame up, and then bought the fibro. I was able to save money because I wasn't going out anywhere, and I wasn't spending anything besides doing a lot of the work myself.
The builder got it to lock up stage putting in the windows and doors, and then I had to hire an electrician and plumber.
Next I ordered the plaster for the interior walls, and I did all the walls. The only thing I didn't do was the ceiling. I put in all the inside architraves round the doors and windows, built the cupboards in the kitchen, then got a bloke to polish all the floors because we couldn't afford to lay carpet. That's how we got the place built.
When the house was finished in Henry Parry Drive, North Gosford, I organized a truck to move our furniture out of the house we were renting from Laurice's Aunt, in St George Street West Gosford, with the help of the boys were I worked, the (D.M.R) Department of Main Roads. My final move was into a brick place that was already built on flatter ground in Narara near Gosford, and this is where my story ends.

I was born in Toongabbie

www.ingramcontent.com/pod-product-compliance
Lightning Source LLC
Chambersburg PA
CBHW061950070426
42450CB00007BA/1115